Vincent's Starry Night
and Other Stories

For Maud

Published in 2016 by
Laurence King Publishing Ltd
361–373 City Road, London,
EC1V 1LR, United Kingdom
T +44 (0)20 7841 6900
F + 44 (0)20 7841 6910
enquiries@laurenceking.com
www.laurenceking.com

A catalogue record for this book is available from the British Library

ISBN: 978-1-78067-614-2

Design by The Urban Ant Ltd

Printed in China

Vincent's Starry Night

and Other Stories

A CHILDREN'S HISTORY OF ART

Michael Bird

Illustrated by Kate Evans

LAURENCE KING PUBLISHING

Contents

Part of the Magic

This history of art begins in a cave in Germany 40,000 years ago and ends on a pavement in Beijing in 2014. In between, we meet artists in all sorts of places. On a mountainside, in a stone quarry and in the middle of a desert, in sheds and steamboats, palaces and tombs – not to mention workshops and studios. We find them painting and drawing on rocks and walls, on wood, canvas and paper. They make sculptures out of stone, metal, clay, wire and even porridge. They patiently set thousands of minuscule mosaic pieces in plaster, join together fragments of coloured glass or bottletops, tear up newspapers and take photographs. Why do artists spend their days doing things like this? Every artist in this book might give you a different answer.

Their answer would depend on when and where they lived. What would the carvers and painters of Ice Age Europe have said? They might not have had a word like 'art' to describe what they were doing, but that doesn't matter. These early people became skilled in making things that must have seemed magical. It is always a kind of magic when ideas and dreams turn into objects and images that everyone can touch and see and live with. Today we don't hunt mammoths, but we still have a strong desire to connect the invisible life of our thoughts and feelings with with the world outside. For many things that can't be expressed in words (or not very well), art is our language.

Works of art put us in touch with the people who made them, even when they lived in distant times and places. But because artists' lives and the way people think about art have changed with time, there's always a bit of mystery. What was it really like to be a Roman wall-painter or a medieval Islamic scribe or a Victorian photographer? Woven through the stories in this book are lots of facts about art –

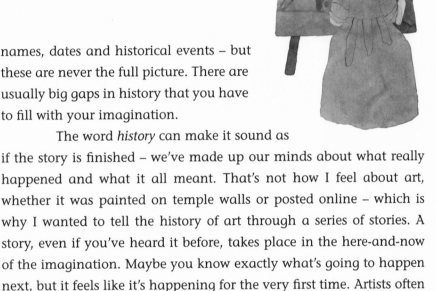

names, dates and historical events – but these are never the full picture. There are usually big gaps in history that you have to fill with your imagination.

The word *history* can make it sound as if the story is finished – we've made up our minds about what really happened and what it all meant. That's not how I feel about art, whether it was painted on temple walls or posted online – which is why I wanted to tell the history of art through a series of stories. A story, even if you've heard it before, takes place in the here-and-now of the imagination. Maybe you know exactly what's going to happen next, but it feels like it's happening for the very first time. Artists often say that, however much experience they've got, when they take the first step in making a new piece of work, they are setting out for an unknown destination.

Some of the artists in this book created pictures or sculptures of a kind that no one had made before. Others make us see ordinary things with fresh eyes. All of them have made works of art that, for me, have a presence all of their own. When I see them or think about them, it's like stepping through a door, breathing a different atmosphere.

For artists, and for the rest of us who look at art and want to understand it, art can feel intensely close and at the same time far away – both familiar and strange. It's tempting to think, 'If only I understood this work of art properly, it would seem more *normal*.' But I never want art to lose its strangeness. It is part of the magic.

– MB

Caves to Civilisations

40,000–20 BCE

Human beings looking more or less like us have been around for maybe 200,000 years. But people didn't begin to make art until about 50,000 years ago. It seems that making art – taking raw material and using it to carve or model or paint an image – was part of a big step in human evolution. It was part of our ability to imagine and invent, and to turn those ideas into something real – an object or a picture that did not exist before. The first art that we know much about was made by people who lived in northern Europe during the last Ice Age.

Some of the most far-reaching changes ever to affect the way people live happened between the Ice Age and rise of the Roman Empire. Discovering how to plant crops and keep livestock didn't lead to great art, but it did lead to towns and eventually cities where there was lots of work for specialised painters and sculptors. The word 'civilisation' comes from the Latin word *civis*, meaning 'a citizen'.

Works of art – from carved reindeer bones, to paintings of animals on cave walls, to stone statues and decorated tombs – tell us more than anything else about how people lived and thought thousands of years ago. It is because of artists that we still have such a vivid picture of the early civilisations of Egypt, Greece, Rome and China, though the ancient Egyptians, Greeks, Romans and Chinese are long gone.

Lion Man
From Stadel Cave, Germany,
about 40,000–35,000 BCE

1
Lion Man
The First Artists

Meet the Lion Man. Firelight flickers on his glossy lion face. His eyes seem to widen. His mouth seems to smile. Will he spring at you, lips peeled back from big teeth, snarling? Or will he drop his shoulders and open his mouth wide for a deep, long laugh with you, his friend?

It is impossible to tell. It is impossible to know if a real lion is prowling out there, in the dense darkness beyond the flames and the shadows. It is a dark that has no edge to it, like sailing in the middle of an endless ocean at night. Above, the cold sky glitters with a snowstorm of silver sparks.

Some things, though, you can be certain of. Whatever you need, you have to make it yourself. Whatever you eat, you must find or catch.

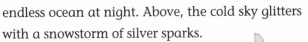

In this cold land, no one survives without clothes made from animal skins, sewn with bone needles that take hours to shape and sharpen. Reindeer hides or fox skins, with the soft fur worn on the inside, keep you warm and alive. Hare skins are even softer and good for children's clothes. Everyone helps – hunting, sewing, cooking. Chipping away at flint pebbles to make arrows, axes, blades and tools for every kind of job that has to be done. And someone has to make sure the fire never goes out. On a winter night like this, how would it ever get lit again?

This is Europe, forty thousand years ago. Half of Britain and all of Scandinavia are covered in ice sheets, many metres deep. Further south, in the land that is now France and Germany, the climate is like Siberia. In summer the ground thaws and plants flower quickly. If you know where to look, you can gather fruit and dig up plant roots that are good to eat.

There aren't many people. Small groups set up camps and shelters. They stay in one place for as long as they can find food there. Then they move on. There are fierce cave lions, which prey on bear cubs and reindeer. Herds of mammoths wander through the bare plains and valleys, like hairy hills on legs. You wouldn't want to get too close to their strong, curving tusks. Working together, a party of hunters can trap and kill one of these big beasts. But lions and mammoths still don't have to worry too much about what humans can do to them. This is their kingdom.

Almost as soon as summer comes, the warmth begins to fade away again. Humans share the deep darkness of winter nights with wolves and bears as well as lions. Life burns away here as fast and bright as a fire. You'd be lucky to see your thirtieth birthday – though with no clocks or calendars, you would never be sure when your birthday was! There are no separate countries, so there are no borders across the land. There is no writing, which means there are no records from the past to spell out the differences between then and now.

Sometimes the hard work of surviving eases up. There's enough to eat. People have time to do other things. They play music on tiny flutes made from vultures' wing bones. They dance, they talk – no doubt telling stories. No one knows what these stories were. Perhaps they were about invisible spirits, who made the sun rise and the seasons change. Or about what the hunters had seen and learned on their perilous expeditions.

In the moment when the hunter comes face-to-face with a lion, he knows that either he will kill it, or it will kill him. He looks into its eyes and recognises the same feelings that he feels himself – courage, fear, determination – all at once. For a split second, before the spear flies and the lion leaps, the man and the lion are equals. They understand each other.

A strange, strange feeling. Who can find the words for it? Maybe this is why, forty thousand years ago, in a place that is now called Stadel Cave in Germany, somebody carved the Lion Man out of a mammoth's tusk. This woman or man spent as many as four hundred hours cleverly shaping the tough ivory with sharp stones. They were not helping their family to hunt or cook, but what they were doing was important too. They were turning an invisible feeling into something you could see with your own eyes and hold in your hands. You could dream about a creature that was half-lion and half-man, but where could it ever be found?

'Here,' says the carver. 'Touch him. Talk to him. Watch his shadow dancing. Meet the Lion Man.'

Horses, Bison and Rhinoceroses
Chauvet Cave, France, about 32,000–30,000 BCE

2
Animal Magic
The Cave Painters

Thousands of years pass. Hundreds and hundreds of lifetimes. But the way of life in Europe hardly changes. There are times when the climate becomes warmer and the ice sheets shrink. Then, slowly – so slowly that you can't tell it's happening – the cold and the ice creep back.

It is thirty thousand years ago, in a river valley in what is now the middle of France. There still aren't very many humans, just small groups here and there. They settle in camps or in the shelter of an overhanging rock. Often they're on the move, through forests and meadows, among the wild animals.

Do humans say to themselves, 'We are completely different from the animals. Look at all these things we make with our hands'? But animals make things too, like birds' nests or foxes' dens. They communicate with each other, care for their young and live together in groups. Still, they don't know how to sew fur clothes with bone needles, sharpen flint arrowheads or play music on home-made flutes. Animals dream, but they don't make carvings of the dream-figures you can

see only inside your head, like the Lion Man. And they don't dip their paws in red earth or charcoal and paint pictures.

In the steep limestone cliffs along the valley are cave systems running deep into the rock. You can only reach some of the inner caverns by crawling along passages where one person has to squeeze through at a time. Except for the cave bears, nobody lives in these caves, but people crawl down here to make paintings. They decorate the cavern walls with pictures of animals. Horses, lions, reindeer, bison, mammoths – the animals that roam the land outside.

There are handprints too, stamped or stencilled on the cave walls. Judging from the sizes of the fingers in the handprints, many of the cave paintings have been painted by women. But everyone in the group comes here to look at them – adults and children. They leave their footprints in the soft earth of the cave floor. Thousands of years later, they're still there. From the patterns of the footprints, it looks as though people were dancing.

How do the painters make their lively, warm colours – their orangey-reds, yellows and browns? They know where to find coloured rocks that can be crushed to powder. Some of these rocks are so soft you can draw with them, like a crayon. You can do the same with the velvety black charcoal from a fire. Sometimes, the painters add water to the powder and use their fingers. Or they mix the powder with spit inside their mouths, and spray the colour on to the cave wall. They've had plenty of practice at their art. They have learned how to adapt the

animals' shapes to the uneven cave walls. As they work, a bulge in the rock face becomes a bison's head or a rhinoceros's back.

No daylight reaches down here. The artists paint with the help of simple lamps that burn smoky animal fat. Or they light fires by striking sparks from stones. In the unsteady flames, light and shade shift and judder across the cavern walls. The painted animals seem to move. And when there is dancing, the dancers' shadows run and leap among the animals.

The painters know the animals in every detail. Hunters have dragged their carcasses back to the camp, where they are cut up and cooked. The painters have watched the living animals too. They know how a lion lifts its head to roar, or a horse's neck arches as it breaks into a canter, and the other horses nearby start running too.

Look at the horses' heads, with their alert ears and soft noses, jostling together in their herd. That horse with its mouth open – listen! Can you hear what it's saying? On other parts of the cave walls, painted lions roam and roar. You can stare into their faces without fear, or with the kind of fear that's exciting, because you know you won't get hurt.

With their art, the painters can do a magical thing. They can bring all the power of a lion or a bear into the cave, but in a way that means you don't have to run away from it. In the paintings, the animals join in the dancing and stories and the warmth of the fire. And later, you can hold the pictures inside your head, closer than if the animals were really beside you, neighing, bellowing, snarling. Inside your head, where pictures dance like the flickering paintings on the cavern walls.

Agricultural Scenes
Tomb of Menna, Thebes, Egypt, about 1390 BCE

3

Picture Stories
Ancient Painters, Carvers and Scribes

It's early morning. It is already light, but the sun god hasn't yet lifted his fiery head above the horizon. The air is full of dew. The sea-blue sky is quiet. Later, it will quiver with heat. The ripe wheat crunches as men cut it with bronze sickles, moving forwards in a line. Birds fly up, startled, chattering and shrieking. Out of sight beyond the fields flows the River Nile, wide and powerful. When the men pause to look around, they can see sails, as though boats were gliding through the wheat fields.

Underground, by lamplight, a painter colours in the figures he has drawn on the walls of the tomb of Menna, a high-up official in charge of farmland. He paints the men working in the fields. I thought later he will paint Menna, fishing and hunting birds on the river, with his family, and even his cat!

It is almost 3,500 years ago, tens of thousands of years since the time of the cave painters. No one can keep track of all this time, though people know they are just the latest arrivals in a long, long family line. They go on doing what humans do best – working out how to get what they want from the world around them.

About thirteen thousand years ago, people living in lands to the east of the Mediterranean Sea discovered how to farm. Instead of hunting wild animals, they tamed them – goats, cattle, sheep – and corralled them into enclosures. Instead of gathering plants and berries, they sowed

seeds in a patch
of ground. If a
family harvested
a big enough
patch of wheat,
there would be
enough to eat plus
some to store away.
And maybe enough
left over to exchange
for useful things, like a
water jug or cooking pot
crafted by a potter with
special skills that a hard-working farmer would never learn.

Already, in the wheat fields of Egypt, the sun is beating
down. How unbelievable this scene would have looked to the cave
painters! The shapes in the distance, like square brown boulders
packed together – those are houses. Farming means that people need
to settle down. There are villages, and towns and cities with buildings
far grander than a simple farmer's house. The biggest cities are home
to many thousands of people.

Great rivers like the Nile and – further east – the Tigris and
Euphrates have created silty, fertile soil that produces enough crops to
feed the city-dwellers. People don't just work in the fields. There are rich
merchants, priests and government officials, like Menna. And there are
painters and carvers, who decorate the temples, tombs and palaces.

City life brings more opportunities than life in a farming village.
But it's much more complicated too. How can a king or merchant keep
track of everything? The taxes that need to be collected. The number
of grain sacks in a storehouse. Or the name of the king who built the
temple, which the king wanted everyone to remember after he died. It
isn't enough to say, 'Don't worry. We won't forget.' The answer to these
problems, and others, is the incredible invention of writing.

The first writing in this part of the world began as pictures,
like a circle meaning 'sun' or a curved triangle like a cow's face

meaning 'cow'. So far, so good. But if you wanted to write 'yesterday' or 'the ship sails northwards', the pictures had to work differently. A picture, or a mark, could stand for a word or the sounds that made up a word, or sometimes both. How could you tell? Luckily, although most people couldn't write, there were trained writers, or scribes, who knew exactly how it all worked.

Painters, carvers and scribes learned skills that seemed magical to other people. They could make you see or understand something that wasn't actually right there in front of you. A king couldn't be everywhere at once, but his picture or statue, or his royal announcements, could appear on buildings in all the towns he ruled. The more impressive the images and words, the stronger the message.

In the land between the Tigris and Euphrates, picture-writing gradually changed into writing made up of lines and marks. These signs no longer looked much like the

things they stood for. The Egyptians, however, stuck to their picture-writing, or hieroglyphs. They were proud of the Egyptian way of doing things. Why change it? Egypt was ruled by the gods, then came the king or pharaoh (the closest a human could get to being a god), then the priests and nobles, with the poorest workers and slaves at the bottom. That was how it was, and that was how it would stay, as long as the sun god was reborn each day after his night-time journey through the Land of the Dead.

Akhenaten and His Family
From Akhetaten (present-day Tell el-Amarna), Egypt,
about 1353–1336 BCE

4
Seeing It My Way
Akhenaten's Artists

When they got their orders, the royal sculptors and painters were astonished. They had to show King Akhenaten with a long, rubbery face and a potato chin, big nose and sticking-out ears, a fat tummy and curvy legs. Never before had an Egyptian pharaoh been portrayed in this way.

By the time Akhenaten came to the throne of Egypt about 3,370 years ago, more than a hundred pharaohs had come and gone. It seemed as if the Egyptian way of life would continue for ever. The pharaohs' names and superhuman deeds were recorded in paintings, sculptures and words on palaces, tombs and temples, as well as on everyday objects. Here was King Narmer, carved on a stone used for grinding makeup, whacking an enemy on the head with his club. And here was a gigantic carving of Seti the First, flattening an entire army. His enemies fell like wheat cut down under the pharaoh's war chariot.

Egyptian sculptors had to be incredibly patient. Their toughest metal tools were made from bronze, which is fine if you need a sword or spear, but not much use for carving a very hard stone like basalt. Sculptors could spend months scraping away at a block of stone with even harder stones. They became expert at a kind of carving called sunk relief. This involved cutting figures and hieroglyphs into the surface of a smooth stone block. When bright sunlight slanted across a relief carving, it cast sharp shadows, making it look like a drawing.

For all we know, some pharaohs could have had warts on their noses or hairy ears. But artists always made the pharaoh's face look smooth, regular and, to tell the truth, rather blank. It was though he were wearing a mask or didn't have a single thought in his royal head.

'If they're aiming to make me look like that,' thought Akhenaten, 'they've got a big shock coming.' He insisted that statues and pictures represented him as a real human being. Akhenaten could even have asked the artists to make his nose and chin bigger than they really were, so that his face was instantly recognisable. Akhenaten and his chief wife, Nefertiti, had six daughters. The royal artists pictured them with their parents, playing and laughing like normal children, unlike the stiff, impersonal figures of the old style.

Just like all Egyptians, Akhenaten grew up surrounded by images of lots of gods. But he thought it was time for a change. He outlawed all these different gods, and proclaimed that there was only one god, the Aten, meaning the disk of the sun. To get this 'one god' message across to the people of Egypt, Akhenaten completely changed the traditional figures and scenes that sculptors and painters were allowed to show. Out went the old gods with their heads of cats, crocodiles, hawks and jackals. In came the Aten, which could only be shown as a circle. The circle had rays that reached out, with little hands on the end, touching the pharaoh and his family. The royal family, with the Aten beaming down on them. That was the picture you had to keep in mind in Akhenaten's new religion.

'This must not be allowed!' grumbled the priests of the old

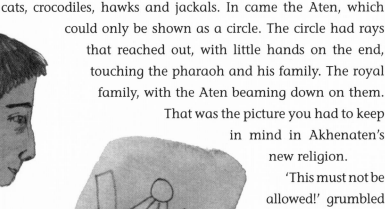

religion. 'The gods will be angry.'
Akhenaten took no notice. He was
in charge, and he was going to do
things differently. He wanted his
subjects to forget the old ways
completely. Everything would be new.

Akhenaten had started
his reign as Amenhotep the Fourth.
He took a new name, Akhenaten,
meaning 'He who serves the Aten'.
He founded a brand new city
on the banks of the Nile, called
Akhetaten or 'Horizon of the
Aten'. He built new temples, palaces
and houses.

A sculptor named Thutmose
had a workshop in the city of
Akhetaten, where he carved the head
and shoulders of Queen Nefertiti out of
a block of limestone. Thutmose made
her look beautiful, with a gentle smile on her
lips, so perhaps that was how she looked in real life. On
her shapely head, Nefertiti wore the Egyptian crown. That
was another thing Akhenaten changed. Earlier pharaohs
had never permitted their wives to be portrayed as their equals.
Thutmose must have been one of the artists Akhenaten and Nefertiti
trusted to do a really good job. He owned a large house, and kept a
chariot and horses, like a nobleman.

Funny-face Akhenaten, beautiful Nefertiti and their six well-
behaved daughters – a perfect family. If there were any arguments or
tantrums, you would never guess it from the royal statues and carvings.
A relief carving shows the girls playing around their mother and
father, while the Aten's rays stretch down as though to tickle them. The
strong Egyptian sunlight picks out every detail of the carved figures, as
though the artist were none other than the Aten itself.

Burial Chamber, Tomb of Tutankhamun
Valley of the Kings, Egypt, about 1320 BCE

5

Life Goes On

Tutankhamun's Tomb

If Akhenaten imagined that future pharaohs would follow his lead, he was wrong. 'This "one god" business – it's not the Egyptian way,' protested the priests of the old religion. But they had to wait about 17 years before Akhenaten died. At last they were free to change Egyptian religion and art back to the old ways. Soon afterwards, Tutankhamun came to the throne. He was a boy pharaoh, who was maybe as young as nine. And in less than ten years he too was dead, from illness, injury or perhaps both.

For Egyptians, death wasn't the end. It was the doorway to the afterlife. Rich people looked forward to enjoying more of everything they'd enjoyed in their lives – good food, music, luxurious clothes and interior decoration, partying with their friends, and any number of servants. Even not-so-rich Egyptians could hope for a pleasant afterlife, provided they got all the preparations right.

First, a dead body had to be properly mummified by expert embalmers, supervised by the jackal-headed god Anubis. The mummification team carefully slit the side of the body open, and removed the liver, lungs, stomach and intestines. They poked a long hook into the nostrils, mashed the brain up and pulled it out. Then they covered the skin in a salty substance and left it to dry out for 40 days. After this, they washed the body and rubbed it with fragrant oils. Now it was ready for wrapping in layer after layer of linen bandages.

Finally, the mummy was lowered into a wooden coffin, which was placed inside another coffin.

In the meantime, a team of workers and artists prepared the tomb. Pharaohs had underground tombs with several rooms. In one, a stone sarcophagus, like a deep bath with a lid, stood ready to receive the coffins with the mummified body inside. In Egypt's dry climate, mummies lasted for centuries without decaying.

The mummification business kept artists busy. For royal tombs in the Valley of the Kings, near Luxor, only the best would do. Their walls were painted all over with colourful scenes in which Egyptian gods and royalty mingled. First all the figures were drawn by the outline scribe. Then they were coloured in by other artists. When the wall paintings were finished, a tomb would be filled with jewellery, statues, furniture and food. It was like a high-class department store with everything the pharaoh could possibly need in the afterlife, including little pottery figures of servants to look after him there.

Royal tombs took a long time to get ready. Tutankhamun's sudden death at such a young age meant that he was buried in a small tomb intended for someone else, which happened to be nearly finished. The burial chamber was only just big enough. It was almost filled by a gleaming shrine, like a tiny wooden room covered in gold. Within it three more shrines nested one inside the other, then a stone sarcophagus. Inside the sarcophagus were three coffins.

The innermost coffin, in which the pharaoh's mummy lay, was made of solid gold. It was shaped like a statue of Tutankhamun in his royal robes. Inside, on the mummy's head, was a golden mask of the pharaoh in his headdress-crown. It was inlaid with deep blue lapis lazuli, semi-precious stones and coloured glass. Tutankhamun was the son of Akhenaten and one of his several wives, but you couldn't tell that from this gleaming mask. Instead of Akhenaten's unmistakable stretchy nose and chin, Tutankhamun's youthful face looked kingly and impersonal.

Once Tutankhamun's tomb was sealed up, no one expected to see all the gold and jewels again. The chairs inlaid with ivory and bronze, the ebony statues of the jackal-headed god Anubis, the golden mask – all these things would stay underground in the dark. When Tutankhamen needed them in the afterlife, there they'd be, ready for him.

It might have seemed like a huge waste. Which was exactly what the tomb raiders thought. These robbers risked being caught and killed, and sometimes ended up buried alive in their eagerness to steal the riches of royal tombs. Over the years, thieves managed to break into many tombs in the Valley of the Kings. They had a go at Tutankhamun's, but for some reason they failed to crack the inner chamber where the pharaoh's mummy lay in state. The seal on the chamber remained unbroken for more than three thousand years.

Vase for Wine with Scenes from Greek Myths
From Greece, about 575–560 BCE

6
Travellers' Tales
Kleitias the Vase Painter

To the north-west of Egypt, ten or twelve days' sailing across the Mediterranean Sea, islands rise out of the waves. Cliffs like giants hunch in the water. Valleys stretch inland, lined with shadowy pine woods and silver-green olive groves. Beyond the islands lies mainland Greece. In Tutankhamun's time, this land was ruled by warrior kings who lived in hilltop palaces. Friends or enemies, the people here spoke a common language, which sounded strange to Egyptian ears.

As time went on, more and more ships criss-crossed the Mediterranean, from Egypt to Crete and Greece to Italy. They carried jars of wine and cedar oil, lumps of copper and gold, weapons, jewellery and beautifully painted pots. There seemed no end to the useful and wonderful things that arrived from across the sea. Merchants and travellers swapped incredible stories. Some had sailed beyond the setting sun. Others had been attacked by a six-headed monster – or so they claimed!

It is about 2,600 years before the present day, and the warrior kings are long gone. Greece has become a land of small cities. The most important buildings aren't palaces any more – or not the palaces of human kings. They are the temples, the special houses the Greeks build for their gods.

The Greeks think of their gods as looking just like people, only bigger, stronger and more beautiful. Inside the temples they put

statues, as though the god actually lives there. As cities become bigger and richer, people replace their old temples. Instead of wooden posts and planks, they use marble, carved into tall columns that glitter in the sun. Building and decorating these marble temples creates plenty of work for architects and sculptors.

The Greek gods and goddesses behave like people too. They quarrel, cheat and fall in love – sometimes with humans. Once there were men and women, so the stories tell, who had a god for a parent, like the hero Herakles. He was the son of Zeus, the thunderbolt-hurling King of the Gods. How different from the Egyptians! The Egyptian Aten was more mysterious and powerful than any Greek god, but you couldn't imagine it talking to you or having a family.

Even more enthralling than myths about the gods are tales of heroes from the age of the warrior kings. There was King Agamemnon of Mycenae, who waged a ten-year war against the city of Troy. Or Theseus, Prince of Athens, who fought the Minotaur. This bull-headed monster lurked in the dark labyrinth beneath the palace of King Minos of Crete, eating young men and women, until Theseus killed it.

Like many Greek artists, the vase-painter Kleitias knows lots of these stories by heart. In his workshop in Athens, he paints pictures on pottery wine vases, cups and bowls. First the potter Ergotimos takes a lump of clay and shapes it on his wheel into an elegant pot. When the clay has dried out, Kleitias draws pictures on its sides with a stick of charcoal. Then, using a brush, he paints the pictures with very fine clay mixed with water. The pot goes into a kiln, where the heat turns Kleitias's pictures black and the rest of the pot a lovely shiny red.

Kleitias and the other vase-painters in Athens compete with each other. They take a familiar story and give it an unexpected twist, adding details no one has thought of before. Unlike most Egyptian artists and craftsmen, they sign their names. What's the point of being an expert painter if you don't get the credit for it?

Kleitias has decorated this big wine vase with no less than two hundred figures. Here are scenes from the Trojan War and the story of Theseus and the Minotaur. Look, just under the rim, there's a rowing boat coming into shore. The oarsmen have all jumped up, waving their arms, wild with excitement at Theseus's success. One of them has leapt into the sea. He's swimming furiously to get to the beach, where the victory party has started. It's as though Kleitias had seen it with his own eyes.

The guests at a drinking party enjoy talking about the painted stories and boasting about their own prize pots. 'See that,' the host points to the swimming figure. 'That's a brilliant touch. My wine vase is the best piece of work Kleitias has ever done.'

'Is that so, my friend?' a guest leans over, his cheeks pink with wine. 'What about the one I've got with the amazing picture of Athena being born, straight out of Zeus's head?'

With its silver mines and busy port, Athens is thriving. Maybe it's thanks to the goddess Athena, who takes good care of her people. Her temple stands on the Acropolis, a rocky outcrop in the city centre. It is time for Athenians to honour the goddess who has made their city the greatest in Greece.

Head of a Horse
From the Parthenon, Athens, Greece,
438–432 BCE

7
Big Ideas
Phidias and the Parthenon

Work begins early in the potters' district of Athens. Woodsmoke from the kilns drifts through the dawn streets. Above the eastern horizon the clouds are turning pink. Rosy light touches the highest point of the Acropolis, where the Parthenon – the new marble temple of Athena – glows inside a wooden cage of scaffolding.

For nine years Athenians have watched the colossal building growing slowly, on top of the huge, flat-topped rock of the Acropolis. Five years ago, the roof finally went on. Now comes the very last bit: the sculptures of the gods. These are being installed at either end, in the triangular spaces under the slope of the roof. You can't see them too clearly from the ground, but when you get close, it's like coming face-to-face with the gods themselves.

Workers climb ladder after ladder to reach the highest platform. From the top, they look out across the city. Far below, the harbour is packed with sailing ships, tiny as children's toys. This morning they don't pick up their tools right away. First, they've been told, there are going to be speeches.

And here to greet them is Phidias. They all know who he is, this famous sculptor who is in charge of the sculptures on the temple, though it's not often they get so close to him. His broad shoulders are draped in a tunic of finest linen, but his hands are strong and rough-skinned from handling clay and stone and sculptor's tools.

'Is everyone ready?' Phidias asks.

The foreman nods.

'My friend here,' says Phidias, turning towards the man beside him, 'needs no introduction. Let's give a warm welcome to the great Pericles!'

After the cheering and stamping, it goes quiet. Is this really Pericles, right here on the platform? He's the Big Man in this city. On the battlefield, in the council chamber, Pericles is the one who makes things happen. It's on his orders that the ancient sanctuary of Athena has been turned into a huge building site. He thanks them all, and makes a polite sign to Phidias that means 'You go first.'

Phidias points to the carved figures behind him. He explains how he and his team have laboured to create this family of marble gods for Athens, where they will watch over the city forever. As he speaks, he strokes the muzzle of a marble horse as though it were alive.

'See here? These are the horses of Helios's chariot, drawing the sun from beneath the waves, up into the sky. In the middle, Athena is born, fully armed, from the head of Zeus. And in the opposite corner – look.' Twenty heads turn. 'The horses of the moon goddess. All night they've been pulling Selene's chariot through the sky. They're exhausted. See?'

How have the sculptors done this? The moon-horses' skin strains with tiredness. Their nostrils flare. You can almost hear them panting, see the foamy flecks of sweat. And yet they're just stone, like the rest of this building. Stone that breaks your back and rubs your palms gritty and dry.

The workers are used to having Phidias order them around. He knows how to run this kind of show. But they didn't realise that, all the time, he was also preparing this magic. They gaze at the delicate folds of the goddesses' dresses – so delicate you'd think the slightest breeze would move them. Yet they too have been carved from stone.

It's Pericles's turn. To look at him, you'd expect him to sound posh. But once he starts talking, you want to keep on listening. He makes you feel part of something important. This is more than a new temple. It is the greatest temple the world has ever seen. And you have built it, stone on stone.

'I have never felt prouder of my fellow Athenians or more humble as a mere mortal than I do this morning,' he's saying. 'Thanks to all your hard work, and to the incredible skill of my friend Phidias, we can all share this moment in the company of the gods.'

There's more cheering. Then it's time to get on. Some of the sculptures still need moving into position. Later today the painters will arrive to add bright colours to their faces and robes.

Phidias and Pericles start to descend the ladders. For a while you hear them joking and chatting.

'How does that poem go?' shouts Phidias. '"As Helios rides in his chariot …"'

'"… his eyes gaze from his golden helmet,"' Pericles shouts back.

Before long their voices are drowned out by the thud of mallets and clink of chisels as the foreman sings out his instructions on the high platform.

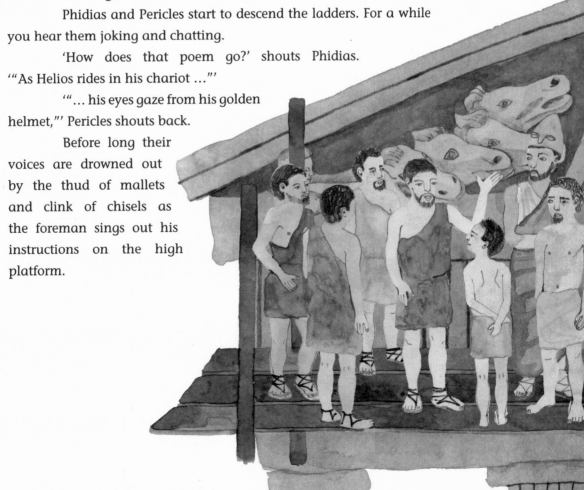

Athens

Greece (about 432 BCE)

The Parthenon is a temple that sits on a rocky hill overlooking the modern city of Athens. The Parthenon is part of a group of ancient buildings in Athens called the Acropolis.

Distant views
To the west, the Parthenon looks out over the Aegean Sea.

Celebrating Athena
The sculptures in the pediments (triangular parts of the roof) tell the story of Athena's birth and of her contest with Poseidon, god of the sea, to decide who would be the patron of Athens.

Success story
Pericles wanted the Parthenon to be a proud symbol of Athens's success as well as a sacred building. It was built on the site of a temple that had been destroyed by the Persian army.

A precious statue
Phidias not only planned the sculptures on the outside of the Parthenon, he also created a gigantic statue of Athena to go inside. It was made from tonnes of gold and ivory.

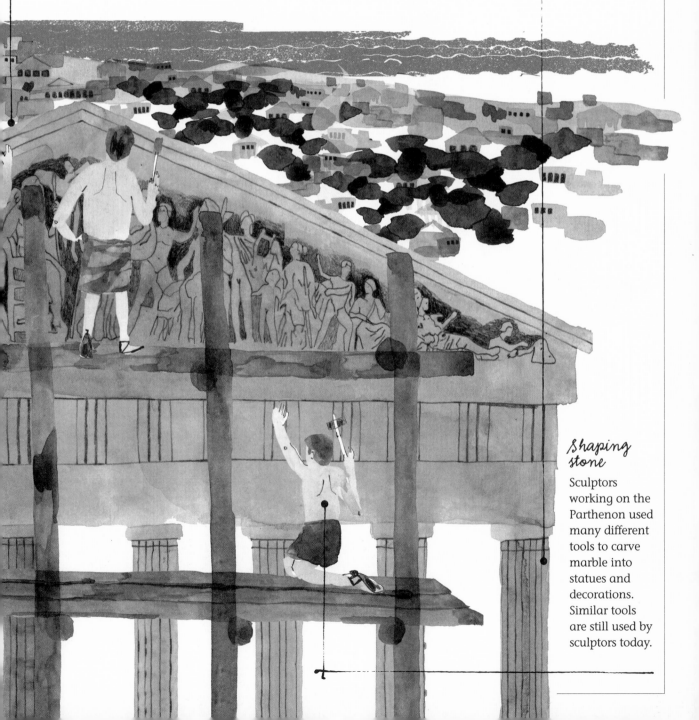

Athena's house

The Greek word Parthenon means 'House of the Virgin'. This was one of the names of the goddess Athena. The city of Athens was named after her.

Reminder of the past

The Parthenon was a stone building, but it was built to look like the simple wooden houses that had once served as temples. Instead of wooden posts, it had marble pillars.

Shaping stone

Sculptors working on the Parthenon used many different tools to carve marble into statues and decorations. Similar tools are still used by sculptors today.

Terracotta Army
Xi'an, China, 228–210 BCE

8

The Warrior Factory

Qin Shi Huang's Craftsmen

Foreman Jiang could not explain the sinking feeling in his heart. It should have been a day to celebrate. This morning the Superintendent of Works had been present to watch Jiang put the finishing touches to the last of the clay warriors. It was ten years since the first life-size warrior left his workshop to be fired in the kiln. Since then, Jiang and his team had made more than a hundred. Each tiny detail had to be perfect – the overlapping platelets of armour, the chinstraps, the boot ties. You were expected to model every statue as though it was your life's work. Then you had to do the same thing again. And again.

Jiang's team was one of 70 teams, whose job was to produce a whole army of clay warriors. The fires in the kilns never stopped burning. The warriors marched out, hardened into terracotta. Painted and armed with real weapons, more than seven thousand of them would guard the tomb of Emperor Qin Shi Huang.

The emperor's mighty armies had conquered all the neighbouring kingdoms to create the great empire of Qin, or China. As a result he had many enemies. The terracotta warriors would protect his dead body, repulsing the attacks of vengeful spirits. Even after he was dead, the emperor would rule an underground empire. He would have a vast palace peopled with terracotta courtiers

[43]

and entertainers, pleasure gardens and canals flowing with mercury instead of water. Some said that the emperor got the idea of making life-size statues from travellers returning from the far west, where they'd seen bronze statues of a famous Greek king called Alexander the Great.

Jiang was modest, but he was proud of his team. They had made hardly any mistakes. Only one statue had shattered in the kiln. No one had been put to death for shoddy craftsmanship. 'The emperor will reward you,' the superintendent smiled. Jiang didn't trust him. It was the smile of a man who no longer has a use for you.

For years the superintendent had sent other foremen to learn from the way Jiang modelled the soldiers' faces. An assistant would bring him a hollow head that had been made from yellow clay in a mould. On to this Jiang added layers of finer clay, silky and smooth. With quick strokes of a wooden scraper or his thumb he formed the arched eyebrows, the elegant moustaches and beards, all the features that make one face different from another. The clay came alive in his hands.

Usually Jiang had to imagine the soldiers' faces. But sometimes an officer came to his workshop to have his real-life portrait modelled. Jiang didn't mind the way the officers' haughty eyes looked straight through him as if he did not exist. While they posed, he studied their expressions carefully. And not all the officers were snooty. Recently one of them had chatted with him in a very friendly way about his home village in Yunmeng, and his wife and young son.

This afternoon Jiang heard unfamiliar sounds in the courtyard outside the workshops. Soldiers were giving orders. 'Your work here is finished. Pack up! Get ready to leave!' He supposed that the soldiers were just doing as they had been told. Still, it did not feel like much of a reward.

'Aha! I have found you, Foreman Jiang.'

The voice made Jiang jump. But it was only the friendly officer from Yunmeng.

'I've been looking everywhere for you. Here.' The officer reached inside his tunic and drew out a small parcel, wrapped in a scrap of silk.

'I told my wife about the wonderful portrait you made of me. She sent you this. What do you think?'

Jiang unwrapped the parcel. It contained a little clay figure of a soldier – obviously the work of the officer's young son. The face was like a small flat cake, with nose, mouth and eyes crudely drawn. The armour was made by criss-cross scratches.

Outside a soldier yelled, 'You must all assemble outside the superintendent's office at dawn tomorrow.'

'What is happening?' asked Jiang anxiously.

The officer glanced over his shoulder. His voice dropped to a whisper. 'The emperor has decreed that you craftsmen must keep the warriors company in his tomb. Take my advice. Go as far away as you can, quickly, before sunrise.'

When it was dark, Foreman Jiang packed his wooden scrapers and a few other belongings and slipped out of the workshop. He walked until he was far from the emperor's tomb. Behind him he could still see the lights of the kilns and the workmen's huts. He thought of the deep, long pits where thousands of terracotta soldiers stared fiercely into the night. Pulling his cloak around him, he hurried on.

Emperor Augustus
From Rome, about 20 BCE

9
A Tall Order
The Sculptor and the Emperor

Emperor Qin Shi Huang was determined that no other ruler would ever assemble an underground army to rival his. This is why he commanded all the foremen and their assistants to be entombed with the terracotta warriors they had made. But he was not by any means the last emperor to believe in the mysterious power of statues.

Around 2,200 years ago, while Qin Shi Huang's real-life army carved its blood-soaked path through neighbouring kingdoms, the city of Rome in Italy was becoming the centre of another empire. Over the next two hundred years the invincible Roman army conquered much of Europe as well as North Africa and the lands to the east of the Mediterranean Sea. Rome grew far richer, bigger and more powerful than Athens or any other city of the Greeks.

As far as fighting, governing, trading, building and generally sorting out the world were concerned, Romans considered themselves second to none. When it came to art, however, they admitted that they couldn't rival the famous Greek artists of past ages. The next best thing was to collect Greek art. Bronze statues were sent by the shipload from Greece to Rome, where they fetched high prices.

Rich Romans knew how to impress their guests. Instead of standing in temples, statues of Greek gods now watched over Roman dinner parties and gardens. Such was the demand for these statues that many copies were made. Sometimes this was done by making a mould from the statue and filling it with bronze. Or a sculptor could measure a statue in lots of places, then copy the measurements on to a block of marble, ready for carving.

For their part, Roman leaders were experts in how to impress their subjects. 'One thing we've learned from those old Greek chaps,' reflected Emperor Augustus, 'is how to make us humans look as powerful as gods. I'll have my portrait done in the Greek style.'

Not surprisingly, the sculptors who made the best copies of Greek statues were often Greek. 'Fetch me that sculptor – whatsisname – the chap from Athens,' commanded Augustus.

The emperor gave a lot of thought to getting the right look. Like the Egyptian pharaoh Akhenaten, he wanted his statue to be instantly recognisable to his subjects in every part of his empire. Unlike Akhenaten, though, he didn't want to look too ordinary, or too downright odd. 'The emperor should be a role model,' he thought. 'Commanding, dignified, attractive. And strong, of course. And godlike, but in a human sort of way.'

The sculptor was used to being treated like a servant by these Romans. They thought they were so civilised, but they knew nothing of the finer points of art, in his opinion. He brought a model to show Augustus. He'd made it in clay covered with beeswax, in which he had carved the most delicate details of the face and hands, while the bare skin was smooth and lifelike.

'I have based my idea on a masterpiece by the great Greek artist Polyclitus, called *The Spear-Bearer*,' the sculptor explained. 'It combines youthful strength with a feeling of great vitality, wouldn't you agree, sir?'

'Hmm,' said the emperor. 'You're not seriously planning to show me naked?'

The sculptor produced a second model. This time he portrayed Augustus as commander-in-chief of the Roman army, stepping forwards with one arm outstretched as though giving an inspiring speech to his troops. His broad breastplate was decorated with little figures. They represented the peoples Augustus had conquered and the gods who protected him.

Would Augustus like his portrait? The face was certainly true to life, but the sculptor had cleverly made the forehead a little bit more noble, the hair more wavy and youthful, and the ears not quite so sticking-out as they actually were.

'Good work,' said Augustus after a thoughtful pause. 'This is exactly what I had in mind. Thank you so much, my good fellow. We'll start with one in bronze, about this high,' he raised his hand above his head. 'Then we could do with five in marble. You can see to all that, can you? I want one in the Forum. My wife will probably want another for her villa, and ...'

'Ahem ... Sir,' an officer whispered in the emperor's ear. 'Your generals await you.'

'Yes, yes.' Augustus turned back to the sculptor. '*This* high, remember?'

The sculptor bowed. The emperor strode off to the council of war, his sandals slapping on the marble tiles.

The sculptor stood beside his model. It seemed to be waving goodbye to the emperor, as though dismissing him – as though pleased to have the grand, echoey audience chamber all to itself.

Painted Garden
From the Villa of Livia, Prima Porta, Italy, about 20 BCE

10
Enjoy the View
A Roman Painter

Ask anyone in Rome, and they'll tell you I'm the best in the wall painting business. But stuck-up senators and their wives don't always appreciate what it takes to paint a scene the way I do. A scene that will make you forget you're looking at a flat stone wall. Like that dining room I painted for Gaius Maximus. They say Gaius's nephew got up after dinner and walked slap bang into the wall. He thought the corridor he could see through the painted archway was real. And not just because he'd had too much to drink, either!

Lady Livia, on the other hand – I've never worked for anyone like her. She's the wife of Augustus, which makes her the most powerful woman in Rome, and probably the richest. Yet she doesn't give herself airs and graces. You'll never see her in glitzy outfits or dripping with jewels. She takes an interest, listens to what you're saying. It doesn't matter whether it's a general or a maidservant, she treats everyone the same. I look forward to going to work at Lady Livia's villa. It's in a beautiful spot, high above the Tiber Valley outside Rome.

This morning the plasterer is there, putting a final coat of plaster on part of the dining room wall. It's early summer and already too hot to hang around outdoors. I love the smell of the wet plaster, earthy and fresh. Luckily the summer dining room is in the basement. The air's always cool there, even on the hottest day. The plaster won't dry too quickly. Upstairs I can hear the mosaic-makers working on the floor. I wouldn't want their job, fiddling about with millions of tiny bits of marble and pottery. They can't really make their pictures flow – not like a painting flows, if you know what I mean.

The wet plaster covers only as much of the wall as I'm going to paint today. The paint has to soak in before the plaster hardens. That way, the colours become part of the wall, instead of just being painted on top. They stay bright for longer, and they're not so likely to get chipped or rubbed off. You have to know what you're going to paint before you start, though. Mistakes are hard to put right.

The scene I'm painting was all my idea – trees, bushes, flowers, birds – as though you were out in the fresh air, not in an underground room. Where the wall meets the ceiling, I'm painting a rocky border, like looking out from the mouth of a cave. My slave Rufus – this red-haired lad from Gaul – he mixes the colours for me.

Yesterday I was painting the leaves on a myrtle tree. I didn't notice that Lady Livia had come in and was standing right behind me. I nearly dropped the brush when she spoke.

'How do you make those leaves so green and glossy? I swear that I can hear them rustling in the breeze!'

'This is what I use, your ladyship.'

I got Rufus to show her the bowl of green paint.
Lovely it looks, like a forest pool. 'We take green clay,'
I said. 'Then we crumble in some of this Egyptian blue and mix
it with water.'

'I see. And here …' She touched the wall. 'Oh, it's wet!
I thought you'd brought a little bird indoors to keep you company!'
Yellow paint glistened on her fingertips where they'd smudged my
picture of a golden oriole singing among the leaves.

'Here, your ladyship!' I gave her a clean linen paint-rag to
wipe her hands.

She laughed, and I laughed too.

I got the joke, you see. She wasn't being careless. She was
referring to the story of the famous competition between Zeuxis and
Parrhasius, the two greatest painters in ancient Greece. Zeuxis painted
a bunch of grapes that looked so real that birds flew down and pecked
at it. Then Parrhasius took Zeuxis to see his painting. But it was covered
with a curtain. 'Why have you covered it up?' asked Zeuxis. 'Can I
draw the curtain and take a look?' Parrhasius smiled. What an idiot
Zeuxis felt when he discovered the curtain itself was painted! 'You win!'
he told Parrhasius. Lady Livia treats me like an educated man, you see.
Not just any old house painter.

By the time I'd fixed the smudges it was late. Outside the
shadows were getting longer. You could smell the trees – pines,
myrtles and laurels, all around the villa – just like the trees in
my painting. Then I heard it. It's unmistakable, a kind of
liquid sound, stopping and starting, like a kid messing
around on an ivory flute. Somewhere nearby, as if
it had just flown out of Lady Livia's dining room,
a golden oriole was singing.

Sacred Places

800–1425

The Middle Ages fall between the collapse of the Roman Empire in the fifth century and the rediscovery of ancient Greek and Roman civilisation that took place in Italy almost a thousand years later.

During the Middle Ages in Europe, most art had something to do with the Christian Church. Artists decorated churches, making Bible stories real for people who couldn't read or afford books or pictures. Most books were made and kept in monasteries. Scribes and illuminators worked long and hard copying out holy books, along with literary, scientific and philosophical texts, and drawing illustrations to decorate them. Artists were usually treated like ordinary workers, paid by the day, dismissed when their work was done.

Outside Europe it was a different story. There was no 'middle' – more like a continuation of ways of life and types of art. During this time, many parts of the world had only limited contact with other regions. Cathedral builders in Europe had no idea that the vast temple of Angkor Wat was being built at the same time in Cambodia. European artists hadn't seen Chinese mountain paintings, or the lifelike sculptures made by African artists. Christian scribes and Muslim calligraphers, meanwhile, copied out holy texts in their own, quite separate traditions.

Though artistic practices in different parts of the world were sometimes similar, artists were separated by great distances. They were curious and inventive, but travel was slow and dangerous, and it was difficult to share ideas.

The Virgin Mary and Jesus Christ
Church of Saint Sophia,
Constantinople (present-day Istanbul), Turkey, 867

11
Eye to Eye
A Mosaic Maker in Saint Sophia

'Coming-ng-ng up-pu-pu-pu!' The words echoed as though someone was yelling from high in the domed roof. But the voice really came from far below. A tug on the rope made the pulley rattle – the sign that another bucket of mosaic pieces was on its way up.

Corax his mates called him – the Crow – because the mosaic maker could always be found perched on the topmost platform, his voice croaky with dust and shouting. He squinted over the edge of the scaffolding. All he could see down there were strange gloomy shapes. Blinded! He was blinded by gold. The setting sun blazed through a window on the west side of the church. Light bounced off the golden mosaic ceiling, straight into his eyes! He gripped a scaffolding pole and leaned forwards.

'Stop!' he called. 'Op-op-op,' his voice echoed. The rope went slack.

It was six months since Corax had started work on the mosaics that were to cover the ceiling of the great church of Saint Sophia in Constantinople. Thank heavens he didn't have to do the gold – acres of it, made of millions of small glass cubes with gold foil fused to the back by firing in a kiln. That was a skilled job, making sure that each piece was set at an angle so that the gold glittered when people looked up. But Corax's job was the most skilled of all, composing the faces of the holy figures.

He wouldn't
need any more mosaic
pieces today. There was
only one thing he had
to finish. The right eye
of the Theotokos, the
Mother of God. From
the hem of her long
robe to the rim of her
golden halo, this huge
figure was several
times the height of
a person. Even the
boy Jesus, sitting on her knee,
was taller than the tallest man
in Constantinople.

Corax knew the Bible story well –
the young woman Mary who gives birth to
Jesus in a stable. It was a humble scene. But when
you thought about it, if the little baby was God, then
Mary was God's mother. That was why, in the mosaic
on the church ceiling, this young woman had become
a gigantic, awe-inspiring figure. As the mosaic shimmered
all around him, Corax felt as if he had been transported into the
night sky, among the sparkling constellations. Perhaps it was like this
in heaven.

'Eh!' Corax sighed, 'I could do with some heavenly peace
right now. But there's work to be done before dark.'

Making faces out of mosaic was an incredibly detailed job. He
had to use thousands of the very smallest pieces. Corax put together
different coloured pieces so that, from a distance, the colours blended
like a painting. He had given a delicate, rosy blush to the lovely young
face of the Theotokos. And all with the tiniest cubes of glass, marble
and pottery.

He wanted to add something to her right eye – a shadow under the eyelid that would make the white of the eyeball more luminous. The plaster was still damp enough to grip the mosaic pieces. The lines he had drawn on the fresh plaster this morning, with practised strokes of his brush, were there to guide him.

All the time, her left eye stared at him. The pupil glinted like a midnight jewel, big as his fist. It made him uneasy. What if, after all his work, when the scaffolding was finally taken down and the church officials stared up to see what he'd done, the eyes were wrong?

'Please,' he whispered to the lovely face looming over him. 'Help me to get this right.'

One eye looked straight at him. The other looked away. What would happen if he'd made a mistake? He yawned. His stomach rumbled. How hungry he suddenly felt.

It was getting too dark to work. 'I'll worry about that tomorrow,' he thought.

The Qur'an

Baghdad, Iraq, 1001

12
The Calligrapher's Dream
Ibn al-Bawwab

A thousand years ago the city of Baghdad was famous for its calligraphers. Calligraphy means 'beautiful writing'. The calligraphers of Baghdad perfected a way of writing the Arabic language. They produced beautiful copies of the Qur'an, the holy book of Islam, the religion founded by the Prophet Muhammad.

Ibn al-Bawwab was the top calligrapher in the city. He was an old man now, but he still taught the art of calligraphy to young students. It was said that he had written out the whole of the Qur'an – which contains over 77,000 words – more than 60 times.

'Is it true, master?' his students asked Ibn al-Bawwab. 'Do you really know every verse of the Qur'an by heart?'

'Perhaps I do,' said Ibn al-Bawwab. Who was he to boast?

Each time he began to write out the Qur'an, he felt as though the holy words were forming themselves for the very first time at the tip of his pen. He'd take a deep breath and breathe out slowly, his pen poised. A long, clean downward stroke, a curve, a dot, another downward stroke. He wished that everyone could experience the peaceful feeling he got from the steady, flowing movement of the pen.

Ibn al-Bawwab clapped his hands. 'We have work to do. First, make sure that you have sharpened your pens correctly.'

Each student had a reed pen, just like Ibn al-Bawwab's. The tip of the pen had to be carefully cut with a sharp knife, so that the pen-stroke was the correct thickness. The writing ink was made from soot mixed with water. Blue, white and gold were kept for decorating the margins with intricate patterns.

The art of calligraphy demanded total dedication. That was what Ibn al-Bawwab's teacher taught him, many years ago. She was the daughter of Ibn Muqla, the first of the Baghdad's great calligraphers. It was he who invented a special way of writing Arabic. He made a diamond-shaped dot with the nib of his pen. Every

letter had to measure a certain number of dots – six, seven, eight. Ibn al-Bawwab worked hard to master this art. His own father was a humble *bawwab* – a doorkeeper – not a learned man. Ibn al-Bawwab couldn't read or write when he started his first job, as a house painter.

It happened one day that he was up a ladder, painting the walls of a house. On one window the shutters were not quite closed. He could see inside the room. A man sat with his back to him, a board in his left knee, writing. Around the room were shelves containing scrolls and books. The floor was covered by a Persian carpet with a pattern of silvery flowers, like a meadow in spring. 'I want to be that man,' thought Ibn al-Bawwab.

How fortunate he was that Ibn Muqla's daughter agreed to teach him. She made him practise writing each letter of the Arabic alphabet hundreds of times. She showed him how to prepare paper, by burnishing it with a piece of agate. At last he was allowed to make his first copy of the Qur'an. 'Well done,' she said. 'You are a master calligrapher now. Here, sign your name at the end.'

Ibn al-Bawwab set up his own calligraphy school, where he taught boys and girls the special system of dots for getting each letter exactly right.

'No, no, no!' Ibn al-Bawwab inspected a student's work. 'This is careless! I will show you how to do it properly.' Ibn al-Bawwab sighed. As he grew older, he did not have the patience he once had.

Nor did he have the energy. After his teaching was finished, he used to be able to write for hours. Now, in the evening, his servant Ibrahim would come in with the lamp to find him snoring. Ibn al-Bawwab often had the same dream. He was writing, and as his pen formed the word 'tree', the letters sprouted into branches and leaves. When he wrote 'river', the letters turned into the swirling currents of the Tigris, flowing past the walls of Baghdad. The word 'peacock' spread out in a glorious fan of feathers. Then he began to write 'life', and … Well, he never knew what happened next because at this point he always woke up.

'Was I snoring, Ibrahim?'

Ibrahim set down the lamp and shook his head, grinning shyly.

Travellers among Mountains and Streams
about 990–1020

13
Mountain Man
Fan Kuan

Not long after Ibn al-Bawwab wrote out his last copy of the Q'uran, a Chinese painter called Fan Kuan was making his way down the side of Mount Cuihua. He had slept on a carpet of dry pine needles in the shelter of an overhanging rock. It was not the first time Fan had spent the night on the mountain. If you want to understand Nature, he believed, you must touch and smell and hear it, not just stare at it from afar.

At daybreak a thin rain was falling. Now it had thickened into mist. Fan could see only a few steps ahead. Nearby a waterfall boomed as it tumbled into a deep ravine. Fan wasn't worried. He would go where the path took him.

'Stop right there, whoever you are!'

An old man emerged from the mist, gripping a rake, which he jabbed towards Fan like a spear. At his side a dog barked and snarled. 'Don't you come closer!'

'Please don't be afraid, my friend,' Fan spoke calmly. 'I seem to have lost my way.'

The old farmer knew that a demon lived on the mountain,

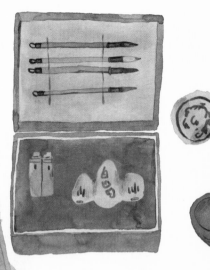

with eyes that spurted fire. When this stranger came closer, though, he didn't look like a demon. His way of speaking was like a schoolteacher's or a government official's. Yet his clothes were all rough, with pine needles stuck in them. His beard was pearled with mist.

'What might you be doing hereabouts?' The farmer still gripped his rake, but he stopped jabbing it at Fan.

'Oh,' Fan smiled into the old man's suspicious eyes. 'Looking. Thinking.'

Looking? Thinking? What sort of answer was that?

Fan often found that people were puzzled that he spent so much time in the mountains. In the city of Luoyang, young artists were always entreating him, 'Teach us to paint mountains, master, the way you paint them.'

'You must study with a greater master than I am,' Fan told them. 'Who is he? Where does he live?' they asked eagerly. 'He is called Nature,' Fan replied. 'He lives all around you.'

This morning, when Fan peered out from his shelter, the mountain's summit was hidden in clouds. He heard the sharp cry of an eagle and the waterfall thundering. He smelled the damp earth and the fragrant sap of the pine trees. People could laugh if they liked, but Fan Kuan felt that the mountain was his friend. They knew each other well.

'No artist paints mountains like Fan Kuan,' boasted the high-up officials who bought his paintings. They hung the long painted scrolls on the walls of their houses, which were stuffed with carved furniture, costly bronze sculptures and silken embroideries. 'You dream about wandering in the mountains like free spirits,' Fan thought. 'Yet you choose to spend your lives in smart offices, giving orders, signing important documents.'

Fan had discovered how to paint a rock face so that you wanted to reach out and touch it. Dipping his brush in ink, he made hundreds of little raindrop-marks. It was astonishing how the soft brush and watery ink could imitate rough, hard rocks.

'Practise the Three Distances,' Fan instructed his pupils. 'Near, Middle and Far. See, in my painting of travellers among the mountains, I put people in the Near Distance and made them very small. That way, the mountains in the Far Distance appear truly mountainous.'

After they had chatted for a while, the old farmer invited Fan into his hut for something to eat. In return, Fan reached into his bag and took out his inkstone, brush and water pot, and a roll of paper. He mixed some ink, and painted quickly while the farmer watched.

'Here,' Fan gave him the painting. 'A gift from the mountain.'

The farmer couldn't believe his eyes. That was him, at the bottom of the picture, a tiny figure holding a rake with his dog beside him. And the pine trees – those ones just over there. And the face of the mountain, soaring into the sky. He felt the inside of his head unfolding in wonder, like a flower in the sun.

Meanwhile, the mist had begun to clear. It would be a sunny day.

'I must get going,' said Fan.

The old man's forehead creased anxiously. 'You know that it is a long journey to the city?'

'I'll be fine,' Fan laughed. 'What did the wise Lao Tzu say? "Even a journey of a thousand miles begins with a single step".' And he set off down the rocky path.

The King Riding into Battle on an Elephant
Angkor Wat, Cambodia, about 1120–50

14
Floating City
The Builders of Angkor Wat

Phirun was too young to remember a time when the great temple was not being built. His father was only a boy when the first stone was laid at Angkor Wat 30 years ago. But Pajan Yan the elephant would surely remember. Perhaps she had been alive when the city of Angkor was just a village surrounded by rice paddies and jungle. She was very old.

Like his father, Phirun was a mahout – a skilled elephant-handler.

'Good girl! Pull hard!' He urged from where he sat astride the elephant's neck, his legs hooked behind her flapping ears. 'Yes! The stone is moving.'

Pajan Yan's feet kept slipping in the mud. But at last the heavy stone began to budge. Ahead, in the steamy haze

that drifted above the muddy road, a long line of elephants stretched into the distance. Hundreds of elephants. Hundreds of stones. At the very end of the line, like a heaped-up monsoon cloud lurking on the horizon, the temple of Angkor Wat.

This great temple was built nine hundred years ago, when the land that is now Cambodia was ruled by Suryavarman the Second, King of the Khmers. The Khmer city of Angkor was by far the biggest in the world, with as many as a million inhabitants. Angkor was a prosperous city. All around, canals and reservoirs channelled the monsoon rains into the rice fields, which produced abundant harvests. Suryavarman's army, with its terrifying war elephants, made many conquests.

What better way to display his power, Suryavarman decided, than by building a temple as big as a whole city? The king's chief architect and his chief priest proposed that the temple should be a model of the centre of the universe. When the time came, Suryavarman – who after all was Lord of the Universe – would be buried there. Suryavarman followed the Hindu religion, so the temple would have five towers, like the five peaks of Mount Meru, home of the Hindu gods. Around the temple there would be an enormous moat, like the great ocean surrounding the sacred mountain.

It's one thing to have big ideas. It's another to turn them into reality. How was the mighty temple to be built? The moat, which was to be as deep and wide as a river, had to be dug by hand. The stones had to be quarried and carved by hand. Thousands of tons of earth and stone would have to be moved.

'Elephants,' said the chief engineer. 'I calculate that with 6,000 elephants, we can get the job done in – oh, I would say 30 to 35 years.'

'Elephants can't dig. Elephants can't carve. What about the rest?' King Suryavarman was nothing if not practical.

'Ah, I almost forgot! We should need no more than 300,000 workers, perhaps only 250,000. They will consider it an honour to work for your majesty.'

On a huge area of bare ground on the edge of the city, men walked to and fro holding ropes dipped in coloured powder. They laid the ropes along the ground, making straight, thin coloured lines. This was the map of Mount Meru and the ocean, and the plan for the walls and moat of Angkor Wat.

Phirun's aunts and uncles had been among the thousands of men and women who dug the temple moat. In the farming season they worked in the fields. For the rest of the year they helped to build Angkor Wat. When you looked down into the moat, it seemed like a river of people, all moving around, bent over their tools and baskets of soil. Then the walls began to rise up. Then, like a mountain, the temple in the middle.

At last Pajan Yan succeeded in pulling her load into the centre of the temple. The air rang with the sound of chisels on stone. Phirun looked down to see a sculptor carving a scene on the temple wall. It showed a man riding a fierce war elephant.

'See, Pajan Yan! You are famous!' he whispered in the elephant's ear. 'Who is that?' he called to the sculptor, pointing.

'This is His Majesty, riding into battle,' the sculptor explained. 'The mighty ocean of his armies is sweeping away the enemy.'

Phirun did not dare say that it was the elephant's name he wanted to know.

There were rows and rows of carved scenes on the temple walls. Some showed battles, others showed dancing girls and goddesses. Others showed King Suryavarman with the lords and ladies of his court.

'What a life!' Phirun sighed. 'But it's not for the likes of us, Pajan Yan.'

Pajan Yan blinked her wrinkly eyelids. Phirun guessed what she had just remembered. On the way back to the riverside, where the large stones were unloaded from the barges, there was a thicket of particularly juicy bamboo.

Angkor Wat
Cambodia (1100s)

Angkor Wat is probably the largest temple in the world. It was the chief temple of the ancient city of Angkor, capital of the Khmer Empire, near present-day Siem Reap. The temple was built between about 1120 and 1150, when Angkor was home to as many as a million people.

Across the water

The moat surrounding Angkor Wat is 190 metres wide and 3 kilometres in circumference. The Khmer were experts at constructing waterways for transport and irrigating crops.

Sacred mountain

The temple was carefully planned to represent the Hindu universe, surrounded by the ocean, with the five peaks of Mount Meru at the centre.

A vanished city

Only religious buildings were made of stone. Angkor Wat was surrounded by a vast city of wooden buildings that have since decayed and disappeared.

Scenes in stone

The walls of Angkor Wat are decorated with thousands of carved scenes, including epic stories from the *Mahabharata* and graceful figures of *apsarasas* or sky spirits.

Meaningful measurements

The Khmer believed that Angkor Wat was built 1728 years after the first 'golden age'. The main entrance is 1728 *hat* (a unit of measurement) from the centre of the temple.

:FEBRVS

Stained-Glass Window
Chartres Cathedral, France, 1194–1250

15
Light Fantastic
The Stained-Glass Makers of Chartres

While an army of workers and elephants laboured to raise Suryavarman's temple, extraordinary stone temples of a different sort were being built in Europe. After Emperor Constantine made Christianity an official religion of the Roman Empire, the Christian Church became a powerful organisation. It was possible to build immense churches, such as Saint Sophia in Constantinople, covered inside with costly mosaics.

Almost nine hundred years ago in France, Germany and Britain, the architects who designed the grandest churches, called cathedrals, hit on a new kind of design. By using pointed arches instead of round ones, and buttresses to support the walls, they could make roofs higher, walls thinner and windows much bigger than before. In Saint Sophia the shimmer of coloured light came from mosaics inside the church, glittering like jewels. The new cathedral at Chartres in France was also full of coloured light. This time, though, the light streamed in from outdoors, through high, wide windows along each side. The windows were filled with beautiful coloured glass. It felt as if the building was more glass than stone.

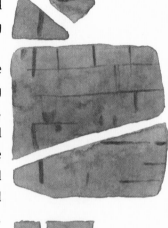

Blue, red, green, yellow. When the sun shone through the windows, the colours touched everything inside the cathedral. The dignified statues of kings, queens and holy figures. The tall stone pillars and the tiles on the floor. People's faces and clothes. In the chilly air of the huge building, the colours mixed and merged. Blue and red turned to soft violet. Yellow and blue became a delicate green, like the breath of spring. Nothing like this had ever been seen before.

The glass was made in the usual way, by heating sand until it melted. Then colours were added and the glass was heated again. Or it could be painted. Small pieces of stained glass were arranged, like a coloured jigsaw, and fixed into a frame with strips of lead. This way, a stained-glass craftsman could make a pattern or a picture that told a story, with the details painted in.

'That man looks just like Dad!' Hubert, an apprentice stained-glass maker, looked over his uncle's shoulder at the round picture he was skilfully assembling from coloured glass pieces. It showed a typical scene from the month of February – a man warming his hands and feet at a blazing fire.

Hubert's mother had arranged his apprenticeship in her brother's workshop. 'You must call me Master here, not Uncle,' he told Hubert.

'Look at him,' Hubert exclaimed. 'Warming his big smelly feet!'

'Must run in the family,' the master sniffed. With a steady hand, he drew the outlines of flames across a blood-red piece of glass. The fire leapt into life. He grinned at Hubert. 'I had another pair of feet in mind, as it happens.'

One by one, the round sections of the stained-glass window were being finished. Each roundel showed

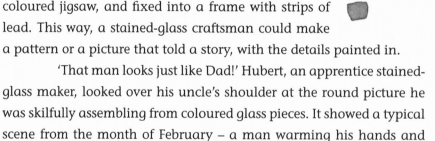

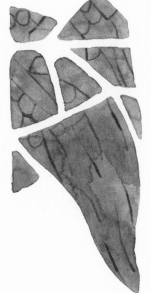

one of the 12 signs of the zodiac, or one of the Labours of the Months. Hubert was allowed to paint the face of the man harvesting corn in the roundel for June. His master's instructions were strict. Hubert had to copy the figures exactly from a book of drawings. There was no room for mistakes. The master, on the other hand, liked to add little details of his own here and there.

When all 24 roundels were ready, they were joined together to make a single tall window for the south side of Chartres Cathedral. It had been paid for by some merchants, who were keen to prove how religious – and also of course how prosperous – they were.

One afternoon the master took Hubert to the cathedral to see the window he had helped to make. There was 'February', with the man and the fire. Opposite was 'Pisces', the zodiac sign with the two fish. Above was 'March', with a farmer pruning grape vines. And high up, right at the top of the window, was the figure of Jesus.

Hubert was spellbound. Laid out on the workshop table, one colour of glass could be hard to tell from another. It was sometimes difficult to see how the shapes would fit together. But here, even in the low winter sun, the pictures glowed as if they had fire inside.

Outside the cathedral, the builders had made a bonfire of broken timbers. Flames leaped and danced into the frosty sky.

'Oh Master, my toes got frozen stiff in there.' Hubert's breath puffed out in clouds. 'I must bring them back to life.'

The master nodded and turned his head away as Hubert dragged off his shoes.

The Expulsion of the Money-Changers from the Temple
about 1305

16
Real-Life Stories
Giotto

The painter Giotto was born about 750 years ago, in a village called Vespignano not far from the city of Florence. His teacher was Cenni di Pepo, nicknamed Cimabue, which means Bull Head. Old Bull Head was the foremost Italian painter of his time, but people who saw Giotto's work soon realised that he was as good an artist as his master. To be honest, even better.

'I want to paint in a different way,' Giotto decided. 'I want to tell stories in paintings, so that people will think "That's how it would have looked if I'd been there".'

Like most young artists, Giotto's ambition was to paint pictures for an important church.

'When people walk through a church door,' he thought, 'they want leave the ordinary world behind. They want to be blown away by gleaming mosaics, light shining through coloured glass, huge paintings of holy figures. Our churches in Italy are already like treasure houses, full of beautiful works of art. How can I do something new?'

The stories painted on church walls often come from the part of the Bible about the life of Jesus. Cimabue was proud of the paintings he'd done in the church of St Francis in Assisi, several days' journey south of Florence. Giotto looked long and hard at Cimabue's scene of Jesus's death. Jesus is in the middle, a giant figure nailed to the cross. On either side his followers stretch out their arms.

'Perhaps they look a bit too much like holy statues and not enough like real people,' Giotto reflected.

As Giotto's reputation grew, someone mentioned his name to the rich Scrovegni family of Padua, in the north of Italy. They offered him the job of painting Bible scenes on the walls of their splendid new chapel. In the end Giotto painted no less than 40 scenes. It was just the chance he needed to put his ideas into practice.

'Let me give you an example,' Giotto explained. 'One of the scenes is when Jesus goes into the temple in Jerusalem. The temple is the most sacred place in the Jewish religion. Jesus wants to be quiet there, to think and to pray. But what does he find? A market in full swing, stallholders selling animals for sacrificing in the temple, money-changers swapping the worshippers' cash into the local currency.'

'You've seen it with your own eyes – in the marketplace in Florence, in Padua, in every town in Italy. I remember the greasy moneylender in Vespignano, and our priest who could be quiet as a lamb one moment and flying into a rage the next. "How dare you come rolling into church as though it were a tavern!" If anyone showed disrespect for the House of God, out they'd go!'

Instead of painting figures like statues lined up on a wall, Giotto imagined the scene in the temple like a theatre. While the big drama goes on in the middle, there are little dramas happening at the sides, in the corners.

'When you watch people's expressions and movements,' Giotto pointed out, 'you can tell what they're thinking and feeling. I wanted Jesus to look like he really can't contain his anger. "This is the House of God," he says in the Bible, "but you have turned it into a den of thieves." He's knocked over the money-changers' table. "Hang on! What's all this about?" one of them starts to say. But Jesus won't let him finish. He's taken off his tunic cord to have a swipe at him. There's a child who has just bought a dove in the market, peeping from behind the long robes of one of Jesus's followers, and another hiding her face. A moment of drama, that's what I wanted to paint.'

Giotto spent two and a half years working in the Scrovegni Chapel. He painted straight on to wet plaster, which is slow work, because an artist can only paint a small area at a time, before the plaster dries out. This method of painting is called fresco, the Italian word for 'fresh' – it's how ancient Roman artists worked too.

People told Giotto, 'It's so different, the way you paint. When I look at that scene of Jesus throwing out the money-changers, I think, "That's how it would have looked."' They said he had rediscovered how ancient Greek and Roman artists made the people in their statues and paintings seem so real. It was such a long time since artists had done this, it seemed completely new.

Giotto became very successful. But there was more to it than earning good money for his paintings. He began to feel something that perhaps no other artist had ever felt before. It really seemed as though, for as long as people went on thinking and talking and writing about art, Giotto's name would never be forgotten.

pudore: † operiantur sicut diploide
confusione sua
Confitebor domino nimis in
ore meo: et in medio multorum
laudabo eum
Qui astitit a dextris pauperis:
ut saluam faceret a persequentibz
animam meam
Gloria patri
Dñs Galfridus louterell me fieri
fecit

The Luttrell Book of Psalms
about 1325–35

17
All Sides of Life
Medieval Scribes and Illuminators

Sir Geoffrey Luttrell is very ill. He lies in his bed in Irnham Manor, his eyes closed. His wife, Lady Agnes, tiptoes out of the room. 'Is he going to die?' she asks the doctor. 'It is in God's hands,' the doctor says, as he always does in cases like this.

When Sir Geoffrey first became ill, he worried that God might be angry with him. He decided to have a holy book made specially for him and his family, to show God that his heart was in the right place. The book would be a psalter, a collection of songs from the Bible called psalms.

A couple of days' journey away, in the city of Lincoln in the east of England, a scribe has been busy writing out Sir Geoffrey's psalter on big pages of vellum, made from cow's skin. This is what books were made from seven hundred years ago – it could take a whole herd of cows to provide the skins for a single book. The scribe works in a writing room. His job is to copy religious books for the priests in Lincoln Cathedral and nearby churches, and for the houses of the local gentry. The words are in Latin, which was once the language of the Roman Empire and is now the official language of the Church, even though most people round here only speak English.

When the scribe has finished, the illuminators take over, filling gaps on the pages with pictures of holy figures, beautiful leafy decorations, fantastical creatures – all kinds of miniature scenes.

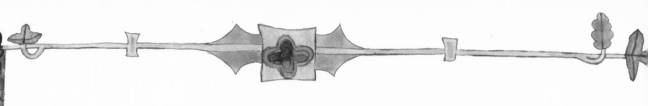

As well as splendid paintings adorned with gold leaf, Sir Geoffrey wants his book to contain pictures of everyday life – farmers ploughing their fields, people feeding their animals, playing music, quarrelling …

There's a loud argument going on this morning in the street outside the writing room. Shouts and insults shatter the illuminators' quiet concentration.

'Gorbellied pig-filth!' a man yells.

'Clay-brained measle! Take that!' There's a crash of breaking pottery. More shouting.

The master illuminator puts his hands over his ears.

'I've had enough!' he hisses. 'How am I going to finish this painting with that unholy racket going on?'

The painting shows Sir Geoffrey with his wife and daughter-in-law. Sir Geoffrey is on horseback, dressed in armour and ready to take part in a tournament. He and his horse wear top-coats patterned with the emblem of the Luttrell family – a silver bird on a blue background. Lady Agnes lifts her husband's heavy steel helmet up to him. First the master had covered the area to be painted in gold leaf. Then he used his finest skill to draw the outlines of the figures and the details of their faces and clothes, and fill the painting with rich patterns.

Robyn, a junior painter, goes to the window to see what's happening. Two men have been fighting. One has smashed his beer mug other over the other's head. 'That gives me an idea,' thinks Robyn.

He makes a quick pen drawing of the fight and takes it to show the master.

The drawing brings a smile to the master's face. 'I like it,' he says. 'It's the sort of scene Sir Geoffrey likes too. But,' he leans over Robyn's shoulder, 'you should make that man's mouth turn down more at the corner. That's it.'

The next day, when master has finished his painting of Sir Geoffrey on horseback, he tells Robyn to take it to Irnham Manor to show the Luttrell family. It's a long way, but the midsummer days are warm and dry. In the meadows around the manor house, men are cutting the sweet-smelling grass for hay. Robyn steps to one side as a wagon heaped with hay lumbers past, pulled by two oxen.

In the cool hall of Irnham Manor he passes the doctor on his way out. Upstairs Sir Geoffrey is propped up in bed, gaunt and feverish. Lady Agnes stands beside him. She beckons to Robyn, who places Sir Geoffrey's portrait on the bed in front of him.

'My master hopes that this painting will meet with your approval, sir.'

The sick man's eyelids flicker. He seems to smile, then he gives a deep sigh and … is he still breathing? Is he asleep, or …?

What a day that was! The tournament comes back to Sir Geoffrey, clear and bright as the little painting. His dappled grey horse stamps, snorts and tosses his head, impatient for the action to start. Sir Geoffrey is sweating in his armour, but through the visor he feels the summer breeze on his face. He lifts the heavy lance. The crowd cheers. 'Luttrell! Luttrell!' He settles his lance in the lance-rest. And he's charging, towards his opponent in the black helmet. Under the horses' hooves, the ground trembles.

Head of a King
From Ife, Africa, 1300–1400

18
Head People
The Bronze-Casters of Ife

Abebi stands at the compound gate. It is evening. Her father and two eldest brothers are leaving.

'I am coming with you!' she shouts.

'Well, you can't come,' her brother Olufemi calls over his shoulder. 'This is men's work. Not for a little girl like you!'

'I am coming with you!' Abebi squeezes her eyes to get rid of the hot tears. 'What a boy can do a girl can do!'

'No,' Olufemi shouts back. 'Go to sleep. It is night time.'

Abebi's father is a metalsmith. He is one of the most respected men around Ife. He makes swords, spears and statues out of shining brass and bronze. Her brothers will become metalsmiths too. Why should they learn the secret arts and not her? And what is this big secret work they are doing for the Oni, the king, which no one is allowed to see?

She has never seen the Oni. He lives in the royal compound in the sacred city of Ife. Here, in the kingdom of the Yoruba people of West Africa, seven hundred years ago and more, some of the most skilful metalsmiths in the world practised their art. In other places, like China, Japan and Europe, metalsmiths made fine weapons and armour. The razor-sharp steel blades made for the samurai warriors of Japan, the armour that knights like Sir Geoffrey Luttrell ordered for themselves and their horses – these were the very best of their kind. But the secret art of the Yoruba metalsmiths was just as amazing.

Like the bronze-casters of ancient Greece, they took a clay sculpture that had been finished with a layer of wax. They plastered clay all over it, layer on layer, to make a mould. They heated the mould until the wax flowed out. Finally, into the gap between the mould and the clay inside, they poured a molten mixture of copper and other metals. When the metal had cooled, the mould was chipped away. Inside was a metal sculpture, with all the delicate detail that had been carved in wax.

Abebi waits until her mother is asleep. She tiptoes to the gate and slips out. It is full moon. She follows the track the men took earlier, with her shadow walking behind her. On either side the jungle talks its night-time talk, rustling, squeaking. 'I am not afraid,' she tells herself. 'A boy would not be afraid. Why should I be?'

She comes to the edge of the sacred city. There they are, her father and brothers. Their big shadows move around inside the metalworkers' compound. She smells the smoke and sees the red glow of the flames. What can they be cooking, out here in the night? Abebi creeps as close as she dare. They are not cooking. They are melting metal in some sort of pot.

'More! More!' Her father orders her brothers. Each of them works a pair of bellows, blowing into the fire until it is hotter and brighter than any fire Abebi has ever seen. *Oagh. Oagh.* The rough breathing of the bellows goes on and on. The fire crackles like a crazy thing, as if the fire itself is about to catch fire.

Her father watches closely as fumes rise from the melting pot and the colour of the metal changes in the night. It glows red, deep orange, then orange-gold.

'It's ready!'

The three men know exactly what to do. Abebi watches as the smoking molten metal, a thick tongue of glowing orange-gold, disappears into the clay mould. Except for little flamy splashes, it is all swallowed up. The men stand back, sweating.

What will happen now? The men sit around, talking. Abebi is sleepy, so sleepy …

A noise awakens her. The men are bashing the clay mould with metal tools. It chips away, and there, inside – a golden brown, shiny metal head. It is the head of a proud young man, a man you would obey immediately if he told you to do something. It is the Oni himself. Down his face run lines of scars, which show his high-up position. His lips are about to speak. What will he say?

'Hey! Caught you!' It's Olufemi. He towers above her. He lifts Abebi up, but not roughly. 'Look what I have found! We have a new helper.'

'A new helper, for another day maybe,' her father nods towards the eastern sky, where the sun has begun to rise, golden-red, like a pot of metal, melted in the fire.

The Three Angels
about 1425–27

19
Snow Angels
Andrei Rublev

It's a winter's day in Moscow in 1427. In the Andronikov Monastery an old monk sits at a table. Beside him are little bowls of bright paint. In front of him, a small wooden board, on which he is painting. Andrei Rublev is the most admired icon painter in the Grand Duchy of Moscow. He has painted icons for many churches. Now he's busy making icons for the monastery's new church. He is alone in his cell. Or maybe not. From time to time, they say, angels visit him.

The new church is built of shining white stone. Inside, though, in the candlelight and shadows and the sweet, hazy fumes of incense, it glows with red and gold, silver and midnight blue. Light gleams on the precious frames of the icons that hang on the pillars and walls, in every corner.

Each morning the servant boy Vanya sweeps the floor and replaces the burned-down candles. This is Vanya's favourite time of day. When he looks up at the icons, he sees the faces of holy people and angels, like the faces of people in dreams.

'Vanya! You slowcoach!' the cook shouts from the kitchen. 'Get over here this minute!'

Vanya doesn't want to leave the icons. They make him feel as though he is being gently lifted off his feet by quiet wings, into another world.

Father Andrei's most famous icon shows three angels from a Bible story. They have golden wings and haloes, flowing robes and calm, serious faces. They sit at a table, where they are about to share a meal with the prophet Abraham. Father Andrei left the fourth place at the table empty, as if to say, 'You too could sit here, if you want.'

Too bad! Vanya must hurry to the kitchen. 'Take this soup to Father Andrei,' the cook instructs him. He gives Vanya a wooden tray with a bowl of beetroot soup and a hunk of black bread. The hot, sweet steam of the soup makes Vanya feel so hungry!

He crosses the courtyard, clenching his eyes against the snow-glare. The fresh snow creaks as his felt boots sink in. Under the eaves of the dormitories, where the snow lies thin, small animal tracks tell the story of the night. And there is Yushka the cat, at the door of Father Andrei's cell, mewling to get in with the half-eaten mouse she wants to offer him.

Vanya puts his shoulder to the door. It groans open. Father Andrei sits under the window, with his back to him. He is painting the face of Jesus. He has painted it before, always in the same way, with the dark eyes looking straight out at you, one hand clasping a Bible, the other raised in blessing.

'An icon is a holy image,' he explained to Vanya one day. 'These images have been passed down from painter to painter from the earliest days of the Christian faith. They are pictures of true things, so we painters never

try to change them, although we all have our own ways of copying the truth.'

Today he turns to Vanya, as if guessing his thoughts. 'Share some of this soup with me. Go on! There's plenty for two.'

Vanya loves the bright pink-purple of the beetroot soup. What if Father Andrei dipped his paintbrush in it? On the little painting table are bowls of azure blue paint and red paint that looks so warm he can almost feel the heat on his cold hands.

Vanya trudges back to the kitchen with the board and the empty bowl. Yushka is talking to him – something about mouse soup.

'That boy,' thinks Father Andrei. 'He sees. Yes, he sees where others are blind.'

A ribbon of sunlight falls across his painting table. And there – it's that feeling again. It's as though he can hear a thrush singing and smell the wild cherry blossom in the woods outside Moscow. But it's the middle of winter. He knows he must not look up.

'Won't you have something to eat and drink with us?' says a voice he recognises. What should he answer?

There's a light, scraping sound on the table. Out of the corner of his eye, Andrei Rublev sees a hand pushing a golden cup through the sunlight towards him.

Great Ambitions

1425–1550

The time between the fourteenth and sixteenth centuries is known as the Renaissance. 'Renaissance' means rebirth, in this case the rebirth of ancient civilisations. It began with Italian artists, architects, writers and thinkers who wanted to bring the achievements of ancient Greece and Rome back to life. They set out to rediscover how the Romans, and the Greeks before them, had constructed their temples and carved such incredibly lifelike human figures, and many other things as well.

While some artists were fired by the idea of competing with 'the ancients', other artists in Europe began to make new kinds of art. Their world was very different from the Roman world and was changing faster and faster. The invention of printing meant that images and ideas spread more quickly than before. Meanwhile, bigger and better ships were making longer journeys. No amount of ancient knowledge could prepare for what happened when ships began to cross the Atlantic more often. The history of the Americas and Europe became intertwined for the first time.

For European artists, there was a huge change in the way they saw their job. Artists like Michelangelo and Leonardo da Vinci no longer thought of themselves as high-grade craftsmen but as ambitious creators and thinkers, like poets and philosophers.

The Feast of Herod
Baptistery, Siena Cathedral, Italy, 1423–25

20
Discovering the Future
Donatello

It's good to be back in Florence. Donatello shields his eyes, squinting into the summer blue. High above, the wooden arm of a crane stretches out. The unfinished dome of the cathedral curves into space like a gigantic broken egg. And that little figure up there by the crane, waving and shouting while the workmen turn the winch – that's the architect Filippo Brunelleschi. 'I'll meet you at noon,' Brunelleschi promised. Donatello looks around for a shady spot where he can wait.

It is hard to believe that it's really happening. Brick by brick, stone by stone, the great dome is rising. Work on the new cathedral has dragged on for 130 years. The dome will be its crowning glory. It will be far larger than any dome that has been built since ancient Roman times. But there's been one big problem. For a long time no one could work out how to build it. Over the centuries the skills of the ancient Roman engineers had been completely forgotten.

Donatello feels proud that it was his friend Brunelleschi who finally cracked the puzzle of the dome. He can feel proud of himself too. Twenty years ago, in 1406, when he was a young apprentice sculptor, he carved two marble statues for a doorway on the north side of the cathedral. Soon after, he received an important commission to carve a larger-than-life statue for the cathedral entrance. His career was launched. And here he is today, the most famous sculptor in Italy.

A load of bricks swings from side to side as the crane hauls it up. Brunelleschi invented that crane too.

What interests Donatello most, though, is another of the problems Brunelleschi has solved. Suppose you want to draw a shape on a flat surface so that it looks three-dimensional. Everyone knows that, the further away something is, the smaller it appears to be. But it was Brunelleschi who devised an ingenious method for showing this in a drawing. Using a ruler, he drew straight, slanting lines that came together at a vanishing point. Difficult to understand? Yes, at first. But painters and architects are quickly getting the hang of Brunelleschi's new technique of perspective.

Donatello has proved that a sculptor can use perspective too, in the bronze relief he recently made for the grand baptistery in Siena Cathedral. The baptistery is where babies are christened, so Donatello was asked to sculpt a scene from the Bible story of John the Baptist. He picked a dramatic moment – maybe too dramatic for a christening! 'The Feast of Herod' is a horror story, in fact.

King Herod is enthralled by the beautiful, cruel Salome. 'If you dance for me, I'll give you anything you ask for,' he tells her. 'I want John the Baptist's head on a plate,' she demands. Donatello imagined the exact moment when Herod is presented with the severed head, and he cleverly used perspective to make you feel that you're right there, watching it happen. The king and his children recoil from the sight, a guest covers his eyes, Salome dances, a musician goes on playing. So many people. Yet in Donatello's relief there seems to be room for all of them. The floor tiles

and the stone arches recede into the distance, just like in Brunelleschi's drawings, so that the shallow sculpture feels like a vast, deep space.

When Donatello and Brunelleschi were young, they travelled together to Rome. They were determined to find out how the ancient Romans created their amazing art and buildings. Brunelleschi went around carefully drawing and measuring Roman ruins, including the huge dome of a temple called the Pantheon. Donatello studied ancient sculptures, feeling sure that he could rediscover secrets of art that had been lost for centuries. Like how to carve a person's portrait – not the perfect head of a god or an angel but a lifelike, individual face, wrinkles and all. The two friends dug up ancient carvings in backyards and fields where they'd lain buried for a thousand years. 'There go those scruffy Florentine treasure hunters!' the Romans jeered.

Maybe they had a point – Donatello has never taken much care over his clothes, even now that he's the best-paid sculptor in the business, thanks to the Medici family. These rich bankers like spending their money on art and buildings. Cosimo, the head of the Medici family, keeps asking Donatello to make new sculptures. He's even given him an expensive red cloak – but can he persuade Donatello to wear it?

'Couldn't you have smartened yourself up a bit, my friend?' It's Brunelleschi. While Donatello has been wrapped in thought, he's climbed all the way down from the dome.

'Too late now,' Brunelleschi grins. 'Come on. Let's get something to eat.'

From a side street by the cathedral drift delicious cooking smells.

Florence
Italy (1400s)

Florence grew up on the banks of the River Arno in central Italy. In the 14th and 15th centuries it was a proudly independent, prosperous city where bankers and merchants made great fortunes. They spent huge sums on buildings and works of art that expressed the new spirit of the age.

Statues for the city
In front of the Palazzo Vecchio is the Piazza della Signoria (Square of the Signoria), an open space where statues by Donatello, Michelangelo and other sculptors were displayed.

Donatello's local shops
The ancient Ponte Vecchio (Old Bridge) was rebuilt in 1345. Like other bridges at that time, it was lined by rows of small shops, which you can still see today.

Citizens' palace
The Palazzo Vecchio or Old Palace was the home of the citizens' council (signoria) of Florence. It looks more like a fortress than a palace – symbol of a strong, self-reliant city.

High sounding

The cathedral's bell tower or campanile was designed by the artist Giotto, who was 67 when he began work on it in 1334. It is decorated with patterns in coloured marble.

Flower of Florence

Building work began on the Cathedral of Santa Maria del Fiore (St Mary of the Flowers), in 1296 and went on until the dome was finished 140 years later!

From the mountains to the sea

The Arno flows through the centre of Florence. From ancient times, the river was used to transport wood from the Appenine mountains for use in buildings.

Portrait of Giovanni Arnolfini and His Wife
1434

21
The Smallest Detail
Jan van Eyck

Far away in Bruges, in the rainy flatlands of northern Europe, artists didn't have the ruins of ancient Rome lying around to inspire them. In any case, did art always have to be about competing with the glories of the past?

'Welcome, friends! Come in, come in.' Giovanni Arnolfini seemed pleased to see his guests. He was soon getting down to business, though. 'I have to go to Italy,' he went on. 'I'm working on – well, it's a pretty big deal. So the portrait has to be sorted soon, if you don't mind.'

'You're a busy man, Giovanni.' Jan van Eyck knew this merchant and his ways. They were both employed by Duke Philip of Burgundy. The duke liked to surround himself with the most accomplished musicians, writers and painters (like Van Eyck himself). Arnolfini, meanwhile, supplied luxuries to the court – velvets and silks for courtiers' clothes, and all kinds of exotic goods.

'What's this?' Van Eyck pointed to the fruit on the windowsill. 'You're moving into oranges?'

'Oh, just a sideline. Try one.' Oranges were almost as exotic as monkeys or peacocks – expensive too. Van Eyck was impressed. He stepped across the room. 'Mind if I look around?'

Giovanni Arnolfini and his young wife wanted their portrait painted in the best room in the house. This was where they would receive guests and keep their best bed. There were some nice touches, Van Eyck thought. A costly mirror with a painted frame, a Persian carpet, good-quality glass in the windows, a brass chandelier. And their clothes. As a cloth merchant, Arnolfini could provide his wife with a wardrobe that would have been the envy of a princess. An ermine-trimmed dress, a topcoat in green silk velvet.

'What's your fee?' Arnolfini asked. Van Eyck wrote a figure on a page of his notebook and tore it out. 'Hmm,' Arnolfini raised an eyebrow. It was a large sum, but he'd heard that Duke Philip thought so highly of Van Eyck that he had recently increased his salary by seven times.

In Italy, where Arnolfini came from, people were always praising Giotto. Arnolfini had seen Giotto's paintings in the chapel in Padua, but he was more impressed by Van Eyck's altar painting in the church in Ghent. Giotto's lively scenes drew you in, for sure, but Van Eyck noticed absolutely everything. Whether it was the skin of a woman's cheek or the grain of a floorboard, he gave the same attention to every single detail. You could tell he had begun by doing tiny, detailed little paintings in books, sharp and bright as jewels.

But it wasn't just a question of detail. It was the feeling that you could reach into Van Eyck's paintings and touch things. He painted on wooden boards instead of plastered walls, using the finest brushes and a special kind of paint, mixed with linseed oil. Oil paint took much longer to dry than the paint used for frescoes. When the first layer was dry enough, Van Eyck painted another colour over it, and another – sometimes five or six thin, thin layers of paint.

'Take a look at your lady's hand,' Van Eyck said. 'It's not one colour. Under the pale skin, see, there's a rosy tint, and on top just a hint of shininess.'

'Are you saying I have sweaty palms?' the young woman laughed.

'No, no! It's the bloom of life. Whereas –' he looked about. 'Whereas that sandal on the floor there, it's just a dull, ordinary thing.'

'It'd better not be, for the price I'm paying you to paint it,' snorted Arnolfini.

Van Eyck shrugged. 'We'll see.'

It took a long time to complete the portrait. Van Eyck started by drawing the couple as they stood in the room. Later he made more detailed drawings of their heads, and of objects like the mirror and the brass chandelier. He made notes of the way the shadows fell. When he'd finished, after hours and hours of drawing and painting, the portrait looked just the way the room looked in the split second when the door first opened and Van Eyck caught sight of himself in the mirror on the far wall. Above the mirror he painted the words *Jan van Eyck was here*, and the date, 1434.

Years later, whenever Arnolfini looked at the portrait, he remembered the moment as if it were yesterday. That crazy little yapping dog – he had bought him for his wife in Ghent, but he was long gone now. And the young woman – so lovely in the painting – her hair was starting to turn silver. Van Eyck had finally gone on the pilgrimage he'd been talking about for ages. People said he was the greatest painter who had ever lived, better than the painters of Italy. And as for the oranges, they were selling as well as ever.

Eagle Knight
From the Great Temple, Tenochtitlán, Mexico, about 1480

22
Fly to the Sun
The Aztecs

The world of merchants like Giovanni Arnolfini was a wide, abundant world. It stretched eastwards as far as China and westwards to the Atlantic Ocean. But what lay beyond the western horizon? As far as they knew, no ships had yet crossed the Atlantic. No sailors had returned with stories of a new world on the other side. There were rumours, of course – a sea teeming with monsters and mermaids, strange lands where you would meet two-headed giants, unicorns and talking trees.

In Europe in the middle of the fifteenth century, nobody guessed that across the Atlantic were great cities, as rich, large and beautiful as any in the world, with wide streets and canals, palaces and temples. Where Mexico City stands today stood Tenochtitlán, capital of the Aztec people. To the other peoples of central America, it looked as if the warlike Aztecs (or Mexica, as they called themselves) were on their way to becoming overlords of the whole region. From the Gulf of Mexico to the Pacific Ocean, from the jungle in the south to the desert in the north, there was no stopping their conquests. During one war-season, the Aztec leader Moctezuma conquered the Mixtecs and returned with a thousand prisoners seized by his Eagle Knights. Another year, the knights brought two thousand prisoners back to Tenochtitlán.

For the Eagle Knights, war was all about how many prisoners they could capture. For Huitzilopochtli, god of the Aztecs and lord

of the sun, the more prisoners the better. Their blood was his food. With every sacrifice on the stone altars of the Great Temple, with every human heart ripped out, he became mightier. The sun shone. The crops grew, and so did the city of Tenochtitlán on its island in the middle of Lake Texcoco. Not so long ago Tenochtitlán had been a little village of reed huts. But who could count its inhabitants now? There could be 100,000 or 200,000 – two or three times more than the population of London in the fifteenth century.

From the shores of Lake Texcoco the city appeared to float on the water, like Venice. It was linked to the mainland by long, straight causeways and crossed by canals. Citizens travelled by canoe to visit friends or attend ceremonies at the Great Temple. The twin shrines at the top of the temple pyramid towered over the city. They were reached by a long flight of steps, ending in a wide platform. Here the Aztecs served up their human captives as food for their god.

The Eagle Knights were young men, chosen because of the courage they had shown in battle. They wore ceremonial eagle costumes, with a fearsome beaked headdress, and feathered wings and talons. Like eagles, who soar so high that they seem to melt into the sun, the Eagle Knights belonged to the sun god. When Moctezuma rebuilt the Great Temple, the Eagle Knights got their own meeting room there. The doorway was guarded day and night by two life-size clay statues of Eagle Knights. Their eyes stared straight ahead, fixing intruders with a deadly glare. Their arms were raised, ready to strike.

'Come,' said the Eagle Knights to their new recruits. 'Say hello to our patient brothers.'

The Aztecs demanded whatever they wanted from the neighbouring peoples they conquered – the most skilful craftsmen, the finest materials, whether it was gold, precious stones, woven cloth, animal skins or the brilliant feathers of mountain or jungle birds. The two guardian statues of Eagle Knights were magnificent. Each was assembled from four sections of fired clay, or terracotta, that fitted together perfectly. The terracotta was covered in a layer of plaster.

The faces were painted. Real eagle feathers were stuck in the bodies and winged arms.

When the young Eagle Knights paraded in their ceremonial gear, they looked as though at any moment they might stretch their powerful wings and fly towards the sun. They carried circular shields embedded with lumps of turquoise that shone like the sky. They wore gold on their arms, in their ears and around their necks. The victims who had been prepared for the sun god's next meal climbed step by step – hundreds of steps – to the altars at the summit. The windblown waters of Lake Texcoco gleamed like knives.

On the other side of the Atlantic, the shipyards were busy. Merchants wanted ships that could sail further and carry bigger cargoes, meaning bigger profits. They wanted ships that might one day sail all the way to China for silk and to India for spices, not by making the long and dangerous voyage eastwards, round the tip of Africa, but by sailing around the world the other way, across the Atlantic Ocean. 'One day, we'll do it,' they boasted. 'We'll sail west and come back with treasure beyond your wildest dreams.'

The Lady with the Ermine (Cecilia Gallerani)
about 1490

23
Under the Skin
Leonardo da Vinci

Leonardo da Vinci is an artist, architect, musician, engineer and inventor (among his many talents). He made his name in Florence, but now he's living in Milan, at the court of Ludovico Sforza. It's been more than 50 years since the dome of Florence Cathedral was finally completed. It won't be long before the Italian explorer Christopher Columbus succeeds in crossing the Atlantic. It's exciting to dream about lands beyond the setting sun, but for Leonardo the most fascinating mysteries lie much closer to home. Is there a difference, he wonders, between direct sunlight and light reflected from a mirror? How do birds stay in the air?

Questions. Answers. Ideas. Leonardo scribbles in his notebook all the time. *Air flows like a river and carries the clouds along, just as a river carries everything that floats on its surface. The wind exerts the same force on a bird as a wedge raising a weight …*

'Leonardo! Leonardo! Please hold Toto. He's impossible!'

He nearly forgot. Young Cecilia Gallerani has come back so he can get on with painting her portrait. And she's brought her pet stoat, the little *ermellino* that Duke Ludovico gave her. 'Why don't you put that *ermellino* in the portrait, eh, Leonardo?' the duke suggested. The creature just won't stay still. Cecilia is struggling not to laugh.

Leonardo has almost finished painting Cecilia's face. The rest of her, down to the waist, is delicately traced with lines of charcoal dots.

Last week he drew her, sitting in the same chair, listening in the same way to the duke's servant playing the lira. Afterwards he took a pin and pricked through the drawing, hundreds of times. He laid it on the wooden panel and rubbed powdered charcoal through the pinholes.

Cecilia is so sweet, so clever – and yes, so beautiful. Leonardo can see why Duke Ludovico showers her with exotic gifts. Many young women would be spoiled by all this attention, Leonardo thinks, but it doesn't seem to have turned Cecilia's head. She brings her poems to show him. She can spout Latin like a scholar, and he's had no trouble teaching her to play the lira, a strange instrument made from a horse's skull that he brought with him to Milan.

Leonardo sets down his brush, taking care not to let the oil paint smear his glossy clothes. He is one of the first Italian artists to paint with oil paints in the way Van Eyck did, all those years ago. If you get oil paint on your clothes, though, it'll never come out. With both hands he grasps the stoat. It writhes like a snake.

'Quiet!' Leonardo says sternly. The animal stops wriggling and fixes him with its mad eyes. 'You be good, or I'll find a stoat-sized spot for you on my dissecting table.'

'Signor, permit me to relieve you of the *ermellino*,' the duke's servant puts down the lira, grabs the stoat and shoves it back in its cage.

'Can't I get up for a bit?' Cecilia stretches her arms. 'I've got pins and needles.'

Leonardo frowns. 'Pins and needles? What do you think causes that sensation? Could it be your muscles pressing against your nerves?'

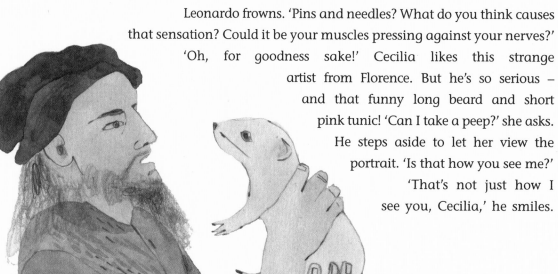

'Oh, for goodness sake!' Cecilia likes this strange artist from Florence. But he's so serious – and that funny long beard and short pink tunic! 'Can I take a peep?' she asks. He steps aside to let her view the portrait. 'Is that how you see me?'

'That's not just how I see you, Cecilia,' he smiles.

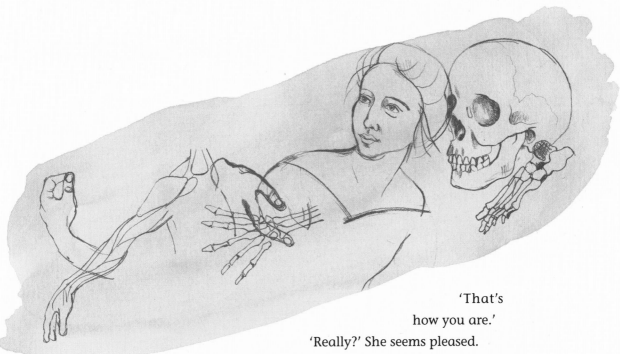

'That's how you are.'

'Really?' She seems pleased.

Is Leonardo pleased with his painting too? He's not sure. A portrait is more than just a face, a kind of mask. It should tell you what makes a person's face the way it is. A grisly image flashes through his mind. He recently dissected the body of a young woman who died in childbirth. How beautiful she was! But behind her waxy skin he found the same muscles and bones that everyone has, lovely or ugly, young or old.

Some people complain that it's creepy, the way Leonardo cuts up humans, horses, all kinds of creatures to see what's inside them. 'Who cares?' he tells himself. 'An artist must look beneath the surface if he is going to paint the truth.' And yet, even if Leonardo has begun to understand how all the muscles in Cecilia's face work together when she smiles, does that make her smile any less magical?

He stares at the portrait. With the tip of his little finger, he rubs a blob of red paint into the skin around the cheekbones. There.

'Toto!' Suddenly Cecilia's beside herself. 'Where is he? Where is he?'

Leonardo looks down. A bar in the wooden cage has been bitten right through. The *ermellino* is nowhere to be seen.

The Great Piece of Turf
1503

24
Work Hard, Be Famous
Albrecht Dürer

'Hey, look at Martin! He's got ink on his nose again!'

It was a regular joke among Dürer's apprentices, but Martin couldn't help it. He loved the smell of printing ink. As he peeled the printed sheet away from the woodblock, he just had to get a sniff. The ink was still sticky. He was careful not to smudge it. Even as he pegged the sheet up to dry, the fresh black ink was losing a little of its glossiness.

Dürer was coming over to take a look. The artist had been chatting to some elegantly dressed customers at the other end of his workshop. Now he had Martin in his sights.

Albrecht Dürer could be scary, the way his eyes bored into you. When he got angry, there was no one more terrifying. But the boss liked to have a laugh, too.

'So, Master Martin Otter-Nostrils. What have you got for me there?' Dürer looked closely at the print as if he was cross with it and pleased at the same time.

'Not bad. Not bad.' He nodded, like a judge letting a prisoner go free.

The print showed a story from the Bible. Mary and Joseph, with their little

[115]

son Jesus, were fleeing from a terrible massacre, travelling through a strange forest at night. Mary and Jesus were riding a worn-out old donkey across a bridge, while Joseph led the way on foot. Dürer had carved most of the woodblock himself, but he'd allowed Martin to cut the thin fronds of the palm tree. Martin concentrated hard. He kept the cutting tool steady along the fine, curving lines.

Martin had grown up in the town of Nuremburg, where Dürer too had been born. Like Dürer's father, his father was a goldsmith who wanted his son to follow him in the business. But Martin had been fascinated by the prints by Dürer he'd seen around town – in shop windows and in the solid, serious books some of his father's friends owned. Unlike a painting, you could make many copies of a print. And because the picture was on paper instead of a wooden board, it was easy to carry around. 'That's the trade I want to learn,' Martin announced. 'Over my dead body!' his father said.

That was in the spring of 1500 – the fateful year when many people in Europe, including Martin's father, were convinced by preachers who announced that the world was about to end. At Christmas, when Nuremberg lay under thick snow and the world still seemed to be going along much as before, his father relented.

Dürer was a hard taskmaster. He expected total commitment from his apprentices. 'If anyone asks you, "So what's Dürer working on these days?" *Stumm!* Silence!' he pressed his lips together. He had become a bit obsessed by the thought of other artists stealing his ideas.

'Because my ideas are the best,' he told his apprentices, only half-joking. 'No one makes prints as striking or inventive as mine.' No artist had painted an accurate portrait of themselves before Dürer did – or so he claimed.

Dürer told them all about his visit to Venice, an incredible city that floated on the sea. He had crossed the Alps, the almost impassable mountains that divided the German lands from Italy. He had met the most famous artists. 'Then I came home, and I became better and more famous than them!'

Dürer took paper and watercolour paints on his travels, and painted the places he passed through. Not heavenly cities or imaginary landscapes, but real places with all their ordinary details.

'You're becoming a good printmaker,' he told Martin. 'Now I am going to show you how to paint with watercolours.'

Another artist might have chosen a religious subject, like a figure from the Bible. Dürer took a spade into the meadows and came back with a clod of soil with weeds growing in it. He licked a fine sable brush into a point and, dipping it in the paint, traced each blade of grass, each dandelion leaf, every single fibre of soil and moss. Martin felt as though he had never seen these things before – not as they really were. On summer evenings he often walked down to the bathing-place, treading these plants underfoot without a thought. In Dürer's painting, the delicate leaves and graceful wiry stems seemed more wonderful than angels' wings.

That evening, on his way across the meadow, Martin knelt down to look closely at the plants – to see them with Dürer's eyes.

'Hey! Smudge!' the other apprentices called as they raced past towards the river.

'I'm coming!' he shouted, but they were already too far away to hear.

David
1501–4

25
Stone into Statue
Michelangelo

Back and forth, two quarrymen pull the saw across a marble block the size of a small boat. *Zhizzh-zhizzh-zhizzh.* The saw-noise merges with the chirping of cicadas in the pine trees above the quarry at Carrara in northern Italy. A warm sea breeze stirs up sparkling clouds of marble dust like restless ghosts.

'Stop!' the foreman orders. The saw goes quiet. The cicadas chirp louder than ever in the heat. 'What do you think, my friend?'

Michelangelo passes his hands over the marble block like a blind man feeling his way. Over the top, along the sides.
'There is a statue inside every block of stone.'
It's one of Michelangelo's favourite sayings.
'It is the sculptor's job to set it free.'

He has inspected the grey-blue marble closely. There are no flaws in it, no signs of hidden veins that could make a statue break in the carving. 'Good. It looks good. I'll take this block.'

The marble will be shipped to Rome, where Pope Julius has given Michelangelo the job of designing his grand tomb and carving all the statues for it.

Michelangelo has been working on the tomb for five or six years, and there's no end in sight. The pope isn't the easiest man to work for, either. Michelangelo wonders if he will ever have another triumph like the time he unveiled his great statue of David. That was in Florence, not long before he was summoned by the pope.

Michelangelo was only 26 when, in 1501, the cathedral officials in Florence asked him to carve a huge statue for them. Another sculptor, Agostino di Duccio – a friend of Donatello's – had started carving it out of an enormous block of marble, but he had given up. The statue was to represent the hero David. Why? 'Because he was youthful, energetic and victorious, like our fine city,' the Florentines said. The Bible tells how a young shepherd, David, fights a duel with the giant Goliath, the terrifying champion of the Philistine army. David's only weapon is a leather sling for firing pebbles to keep the wolves away from his sheep. Goliath just laughs at him. But David's expert slingshot hits the giant smack between the eyes, killing him instantly.

The magnificent block of Carrara marble was the height of three tall men. Michelangelo cursed Agostino. He had gouged deep into the stone, where the legs of his statue were going to be. Whatever Michelangelo did, he would have to adapt his ideas to the crude holes Agostino had already made.

Maybe that wasn't such a disaster, after all. Maybe

this was Michelangelo's chance to prove that he could find the statue in any stone, even one that had been messed around with. Using all his skill, he would make the marble fall away to reveal the strong young figure of David. In Florence at that time there was a lot of talk about the astonishing achievements of ancient sculptors. Well, Michelangelo would beat the ancient Greeks and Romans at their own game. He would carve the biggest, most beautiful naked human figure that any sculptor had carved for almost two thousand years.

For two years he worked away. When the statue was finished, the cathedral officials were astonished at the young sculptor's skill in carving marble and his bold ideas. How had he made this naked figure express so much – the mixture of confidence and anxiety in David's face, the sense of calm and danger at the same time? But they also realised that the statue was much too large and heavy to go on the roof of the cathedral, where they'd planned to put it.

After discussing the question with other artists, including Leonardo, they decided that Michelangelo's *David* must stand in the main square in Florence, in front of the town hall. Builders bashed a gap through the top of the workshop gates, and *David* was wheeled out and processed through the streets in triumph. That same evening, a street gang pelted it with stones – maybe they preferred the statue by Donatello that had stood in the place of honour before. Michelangelo wasn't too bothered. 'It proves that if you do something important, you're bound to make enemies,' he mused. He knew that his *David* had lifted him above all other sculptors of his time.

'Amazing, when you think about it,' the foreman's voice jolts Michelangelo out of his reverie. 'One day you're with His Holiness the Pope in Rome, the next you're here in the quarry, chatting with your old mate.'

'And can't you guess which I'd rather be doing?' Michelangelo's fierce, troubled face softens. He thumps the foreman on the back. He runs his hands once more over the newly cut block of marble. Inside, yes – he can feel it. A statue is straining to break out with all its might.

Philosophy, or the School of Athens
Apostolic Palace, Vatican City, Italy, 1510–12

26
The Art of Philosophy
Raphael

'An artist paints with his brains, not with his hands!'

Michelangelo has a point. He usually does. But why must he always be mouthing off about something or other? 'If he's not careful,' thinks Raphael, 'he'll become more famous for his words than his art.'

It is 1510, and the young painter Raphael is living in Rome. Like Michelangelo, he's working for Pope Julius. The pope has great ambitions for the city. He wants his Rome to be even more glorious than the city of the Roman emperors. New buildings and monuments are going up all the time. Julius is constantly on the lookout for artistic talent. He has hired Raphael to paint frescoes on the walls of his private apartments in the Vatican Palace. Elsewhere in the palace, Michelangelo is hard at work, covering the vast ceiling of the Sistine Chapel with paintings, not to mention creating the sculptures for Julius's tomb.

Raphael is eight years younger than Michelangelo, but already he's catching up with him in fame. People love his graceful, sensitive paintings. As Raphael is well aware, they also find him much easier to get on with than surly Michelangelo. Everyone agrees that Michelangelo is the greatest sculptor who ever lived. But can his paintings compete with the work of the brilliant young newcomer, Raphael?

The pope wants the frescoes in his library to show serious and inspiring scenes. Frankly, he isn't that interested in books. But these days a great prince must be totally in command of culture and knowledge, as well as armies and kingdoms. And what could be a better subject for his library walls than 'Philosophy'? It's a fine-sounding word, with a fine meaning: 'the love of wisdom'.

'How do you propose that I represent Philosophy, Your Holiness?' Raphael asks.

'I'd like to have a gathering of all the ancient philosophers, so that I can imagine they're in my library, doing their – you know, philosophising. Plato, Aristotle, Socrates, Hega … What's his name? Hella …'

'Do you mean Heraclitus, Your Holiness?' suggests Raphael tactfully.

But already Pope Julius has turned on his heel. 'Excellent. I'll leave you to it. I must find out what that mad dog Michelangelo is up to in the chapel.'

Raphael's own father was an artist, in the hilltop town of Urbino, but you'd never have found him discussing Latin poetry with writers or talking with mathematicians and musicians about harmony and proportion. Pope Julius encourages that kind of thing at his court.

Well then, that's how *Philosophy* will look. Raphael will paint groups of thinkers, deep in learned discussions. They'll be walking and talking together in a magnificent setting, with grand arches, marble flooring and statues – a city like he imagines ancient Athens must have been. He might need some advice to get the architectural details exactly right. The pope's favourite architect, Donato Bramante, will be sure to have the answers.

Nobody knows what the ancient philosophers really looked like, so Raphael models some of their portraits on artists of his own time. Right at the centre stands the Greek philosopher Plato, pointing upwards to the realm of invisible ideas. He's represented by Leonardo da Vinci, instantly recognisable with his long beard, bald head and intense expression. Below Plato is the seated figure of Heraclitus, known as the 'weeping philosopher'. Who could be Heraclitus? Michelangelo, of course! He is brooding darkly, his back turned to the others, perhaps writing a poem.

'And where shall I be?' thinks Raphael. He decides to paint himself as a Greek artist, the famous Apelles, standing at the edge. It's as though he's been observing the philosophers, then he glances to one side.

'Oh, excellent! Excellent!' Pope Julius is pleased with the way the fresco is taking shape. 'I've only just noticed that that's you, Raphael, in the corner, looking straight at me. Very clever – and very modest, I must say!'

On the way back to his lodgings, Raphael bumps into Michelangelo. The older artist looks furious, as though he's going to strangle the next person he sees.

'What do you think those imbeciles just said to me?' he demands.

'*What* imbeciles?' Raphael enquires calmly.

'Those cretins, the cardinals. "We think that you should devise some way to conceal the nakedness of Adam and Eve in your frescoes".' He imitates the snooty voices of the two cardinals who have been spying on him in the chapel. No one – not even the pope – is allowed to watch Michelangelo at work. 'Idiots!'

'Shhh!' Raphael puts a finger to his lips. He can hear footsteps and voices approaching.

Michelangelo looks at him sharply, then stomps off, raging to himself. 'Scumbags! Dunderheads!'

A door clangs shut. Michelangelo's grumbling gradually dies away in the echoey corridors. 'Michelangelo!' Raphael smiles to himself. 'You're impossible! You really should try to be a little more – what's the word? *Philosophical.*'

Bacchus and Ariadne
1520–23

27
The Night Is Young
Titian

'What are you telling me? Raphael's *dead*?' Duke Alfonso of Ferrara looks genuinely shocked, but at the same time a shadow of annoyance darkens his face. The duke isn't used to people saying 'no' to him, but he can't argue with death. It is April 1520, when Raphael should have celebrated his 37th birthday. Instead, he caught a deadly fever.

'I regret that it is true, my lord,' his chamberlain gives a deep sigh. 'I received the news from Rome this morning.'

'We must find another artist. Who do you suggest?'

'May I recommend Titian? Your lordship is already familiar his work.'

'Very good. Bring him here.'

Duke Alfonso has spent most of the past 20 years fighting. The princes and noblemen of Italy, including the pope himself, are constantly at each other's throats. No sooner has one battle been fought than Alfonso hears rumblings of another plot, another army on the march, another treaty torn to shreds. Thankfully, the walls of Ferrara are strong, and the duke's foundries produce mighty cannon. When the people of Bologna rebelled against Pope Julius, they smashed up

Michelangelo's colossal bronze statue of him. Duke Alfonso had the bronze fragments melted down and turned into a cannon.

It's not that Alfonso hates art. On the contrary, he adores it. He wants his art collection at Ferrara to be the finest in Italy – finer even than the treasures amassed by that crafty old scoundrel Pope Julius. Blast it all! Raphael was supposed to be painting a picture for Alfonso that would outshine his famous paintings for Julius. He'd already made a start – a scene featuring Bacchus, Roman god of wine and wild living. A god who is close to Alfonso's heart.

'You have big shoes to fill,' he tells Titian.

Titian bows. He already has a painting in mind. Michelangelo, Raphael – no artist could compete with these two on their own terms. But Titian has something they didn't have. He understands the magic of deep, luminous colour. He knows how a painting can come alive with colour, light and shade, like an enchanted clearing in a forest. The sunlight is full of the moving shadows of leaves. While you watch, the spirits come out into the clearing, not realising you are there.

Perhaps it is a good thing that in Venice, where Titian comes from, artists are not faced at every step with reminders of ancient Rome. Instead, they see the continual coming and going of merchants from the east, bringing silks, spices, amber, lapis lazuli. They live in the constantly changing light of the sea.

Titian studies Roman poems and stories about Bacchus. He paints the god of wine crowned with vine leaves. He's leaping from his chariot into the air, like an athlete – unlike any action that Raphael ever painted. Bacchus is in love with the Cretan princess Ariadne. Prince Theseus has deserted her on the lonely island of Naxos, where she hears the clamour of Bacchus and his followers chasing after her, getting closer and closer. She turns, frightened but dignified. Bacchus reassures her that the leopards drawing his chariot won't hurt her. Cymbals clash. A boy-satyr drags a slaughtered calf's head like a toy on a string. And a little dog, perhaps a portrait of Duke Alfonso's own pet, yaps at the wild crowd.

Titian has finished his painting. It hangs in the duke's special art gallery, the Alabaster Rooms. No one else has a gallery like this. The walls are lined with gleaming marble, and this evening the candles have been lit. Titian's colours glow against the pale grey stone while he waits for the duke to arrive. Ariadne's dress, lapis-lazuli blue, shimmers like the sea at night. Bacchus's red robe has the sheen of silk. In the sky is a circle of eight stars – the constellation into which Ariadne will later be transformed. Such stillness. Such rowdiness. Only in a painting, Titian reflects, can these opposites meet.

'This way! Follow me! What have you got for us, Signor Titian?' Duke Alfonso bursts in with a crowd of guests. They've been feasting and they're in high spirits, joking, singing. Servants bring more candles. The court musicians come trailing after.

The duke steps close to the painting, almost rubbing his nose in it. 'This is meant to be me, no?' He swings round to Titian, pointing at the youthful figure of Bacchus.

Titian stares into the heavy, bearded face of a man in his mid-forties. There's a grey streak in the duke's hair. He has bags under his eyes. You have to be careful with these noblemen. Flatter them too much, and they think you are poking fun.

Thank goodness. Before Titian can answer, Alfonso claps his hands. 'Play!' he commands his musicians. 'Play on! See,' he waves at the painting. 'The stars have only just come out. The night is young!'

Life Stories
1550–1750

Through the fifteenth century and into the sixteenth and seventeenth, one new idea led to another. It seemed that every advance in technology could be improved on. Modern science took shape. Instead of accepting traditional explanations of nature, the human body or the universe, scientists questioned, experimented and measured. They found that everything could be understood in surprising new ways, from plants to people to planets.

In India, artists depicted emperors as glorious figures, skilled hunters and warriors, collecting their paintings in books that recorded the lives of important rulers. In Europe, different people were taking an interest in art – not only popes, kings and aristocrats, but also merchants, lawyers and others who had grown rich from their work rather than from land and money that came from their ancestors. They wanted portraits of themselves and their families; they preferred paintings they could hang on their walls at home to enormous statues that would only look good in a grand setting.

The Spanish royalty in Velázquez's portraits and the religious figures in Italian artist Caravaggio's scenes have something in common: they look like real people living their lives – eating, sleeping, chatting, getting older day by day – the way everyone does. Instead of turning to gods and goddesses for interesting subject matter, artists looked to the everyday world, finding it just as full of mystery and wonder as the tales of ancient Greece.

Hunters in the Snow
1565

28
Cold Comfort
Pieter Bruegel

Pieter Bruegel's fingertips feel like icicles. He can't feel his toes at all. The cold is working its way up his legs, along his arms.

His friend Nicolaes Jonghelinck claps his hands, shaking pads of snow off his sleeves. 'Come along, Bruegel! Hunting keeps a man young! The thrill of the chase. Back to nature!'

The hunters have been out with their dogs since before dawn. They have tramped for hours through the thick snow. Bruegel is convinced they're about to die of cold. And for what? They've caught one mangy hare, not enough to feed the dogs, let alone make a feast back home.

Now, at last, they are heading back to Jonghelinck's country house, a big, comfortable old place. There'll be a fire blazing in the hall and food piled on the table, more than you could ever eat. 'So,' Jonghelinck will say, settling down with his steaming cup of spiced ale. 'How are my "Seasons" coming along?'

The rich merchant has commissioned a set of large paintings from Bruegel. He's chosen a familiar theme: the Seasons of the Year. Sitting by the fire in February, harvesting hay in June, ploughing the fields in October … You can find pictures of the seasons and

their traditional activities on church walls, in moth-eaten tapestries and in countless old books. But Bruegel will give this time-honoured subject a new look. He will show things how they really are, today, in 1565.

Snow makes everything seem new. It makes life harder, but somehow it makes us feel carefree too, thinks Bruegel. As they walk through a village, he sees children playing on the frozen ponds. They're bending down, strapping on their ice skates, using stools as sledges. Shrieks and laughter echo, sharp and clear in the cold air. The soft grey sky is weighed down with snow waiting to fall.

When did he last hear such happy sounds? He doesn't often see the villagers' lives at such close quarters. When they work, the work is hard – carrying wood for the fire, loading wagons, hauling bags of grain to the watermill. When they play, they want dancing, singing and games. What use are artists and paintings to them?

Jonghelinck, on the other hand, likes fine clothes, fine food, fine wine, and a fine painting to look at while he eats his dinner. Peasants working in the fields or dancing at a wedding. Those are his favourite kinds of scenes. 'Bruegel, my friend,' he sighs. 'What wouldn't I give to live the simple country life? Hard work, sound sleep, simple pleasures – nothing better!'

Outside a tavern, the innkeeper and

his family are stoking a fire. They're about to scald the pig they've slaughtered. They will scrape the hairs off the pig's skin before they cut it up for meat. This has always been one of the jobs for December, one of the age-old Labours of the Months. Even from a distance, Bruegel feels the crackling fire hot on his face.

He wiggles his fingers, trying to make the blood flow back. He stares across the snowy land. The busy little figures on the ice, the crows perched in the bare branches, are clear and sharp as if they'd been drawn with ink. That's it. That's how he will paint December, just how it feels today. The cold air, the fire's heat, the shouts echoing from the frozen ponds.

When Bruegel was young he walked all the way across Europe to Italy. He wanted to see for himself the paintings of famous Italian artists. Their work helped him to learn about the many different ways an artist can paint a scene. Giotto, for example, included lots of figures and drama. Titian often painted a landscape in the background, with trees, rivers and mountains in the blue distance.

What Bruegel remembers better than any work of art, though, is the dangerous journey across the Alps, the mountains that divide Italy from the north. He remembers the wonder he felt when he looked up at the splintered peaks high above him and down the steep slopes that disappeared into dark valleys below the narrow path. 'We are so small and insignificant, just tiny sparks of warmth in a cold landscape,' he thinks.

'Come on!' Jonghelinck is calling. 'Put your best foot forward! Nearly there!'

Bruegel searches for the merchant's house. As far as the eye can see there are flat, snow-covered fields, frozen ponds and streams. How much further can it be?

'Bruegel! Bruegel! Good heavens, man. Your face is turning blue!' Jonghelinck shakes him by the shoulders. 'And your hands, they're like blocks of ice!' He rubs them between his own. 'Here, borrow my fur gloves. No, I insist! If your fingers drop off with frostbite, who's going to paint my "Seasons", eh?'

Akbar Hunts in the Neighbourhood of Agra
about 1590–95

29
King of the Cheetahs
Basawan and Dharm Das

'Which do you think our emperor loves more – hunting or fighting?' Basawan looked up from the sheet of paper in front of him. It bore a brightly coloured painting of Emperor Akbar on horseback, hunting with cheetahs. Basawan had added a few spots to the outstretched shape of a leaping cheetah. It was about to sink its claws into a terrified antelope.

'Fighting, of course!' Dharm Das, a junior court artist, was assisting Basawan with the painting. He had never been in a battle, but he had helped to paint battle scenes in the Book of Akbar, the magnificent story of the emperor's life. What could be more exciting than guns banging, clashing swords, kicking the severed heads of enemies as they rolled in the dust?

'You could be right,' Basawan sat back. 'But I think you're wrong. I have heard that when our emperor was young, he travelled through Hindustan with a great hunting party – great as an army. He enjoyed the sport. At the same time it kept his enemies quiet. They realised that if they angered Akbar, he would come hunting for *them*.'

Yes, the painting was nearly ready to present to the emperor. Basawan only needed to make Akbar's moustache a little longer. Just the smallest touch of black, like so. He had given Akbar's face a calm, intelligent expression – an expression he knew well. This was how

Akbar liked to look, even when he was meant to be hunting or urging his soldiers into battle.

'So?' Dharm Das changed the subject. 'Are you pleased with my colours? This blue,' he pointed to saddlecloth on Akbar's horse. 'What do you think?'

'It's good. You remember the blue I asked for?'

'Like the sky in Kashmir after sunset!'

'Exactly. Well done.'

Dharm Das learned fast, but you only had to glance at the picture to see that it was Basawan's idea. Of all the artists the emperor employed, more than a hundred of them, Basawan alone created scenes like this. Here was all the excitement of the hunting party – people, horses, cheetahs, elephants, antelopes – and yet nothing felt crowded or confused.

Basawan was the emperor's favourite artist. Akbar had never learned to read, but he certainly knew a thing or two about painting. He had even taken painting lessons. These days he had no time, of course. How could he? His empire stretched from the Arabian Sea to the Bay of Bengal and northwards to the Himalayas. It was far larger than the kingdom he had inherited from his father, Humayun, when he was just 18. He had built up that empire himself. His great deeds would never be forgotten.

The Book of Akbar was being illustrated by his best artists. Before they began each painting, Akbar liked to discuss with them what would go in it.

'You know how we hunt with cheetahs?' he questioned Basawan.

The painter knew perfectly well, but he let the emperor go on. 'The cheetah hunts by sight, not smell. For this reason my servants carry the cheetahs to the hunting ground in special cages. The cheetahs have to be blindfolded, so they don't get distracted. Ah, Basawan! What is more lovely than the ripple of a cheetah's back when it races after its prey!'

Basawan bowed. To tell the truth, he was more interested in the books and pictures that Akbar had been given by a priest who had recently arrived in court from Italy. The emperor was kind to the priest and listened thoughtfully to his preaching, although now and then a frown of irritation crossed his calm, intelligent face. Basawan particularly admired a picture that had the letters *AD* in the corner. The artist was German and his name was Albrecht Dürer, the priest told him.

The picture was printed in black ink. It showed a holy lady with a baby on a donkey, being led by a man through a forest at night. Each part was packed with detail. Leaves, birds and animals, people's clothes and faces. It surprised Basawan that the Italian priest, who never seemed to change his clothes or wash properly, possessed such a beautiful picture.

Later that day Basawan and Dharm Das walked through the palace courtyards to show their painting to the emperor. They passed old Abu'l Fazl, author of the Book of Akbar, who shuffled along every day to read aloud to the emperor. His orange-gold silken robe billowed in the evening breeze.

Basawan turned to Dharm Das. 'Could you describe that colour?' he said.

'Ripe mango?' Dharm Das suggested.

Basawan shook his head.

'Fresh saffron that has just begun to dry?'

'No-o.'

Dharm Das stood still, one hand raised as though waiting for inspiration.

'It – is – the – colour – of – the – '

'Cheetah's eye!' they said in unison, and walked on, laughing.

The Supper at Emmaus
1601

30

Light Supper

Caravaggio

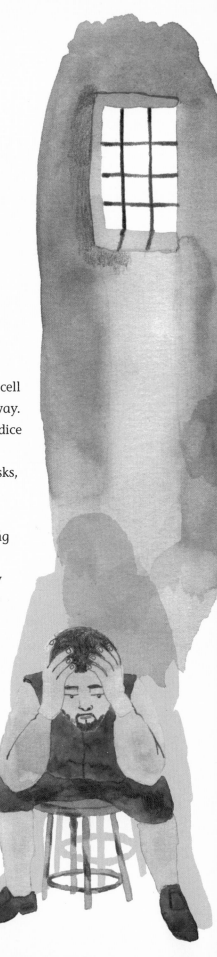

'Let me out! It's a mistake I tell you!'

The new prisoner is making a racket. Luckily his cell is at the end of the corridor. The gaoler shrugs and walks away. He's heard it all before. He wants to get back to his game of dice with the guard.

'Who's the *guappo* you've got there?' the guard asks, shaking the dice in his fists.

'Some lousy painter. Name of Caravaggio.'

'Let me out!' the furious voice echoes. 'I'm expecting a pardon from the pope!'

'And I'm expecting a fried egg from the Holy Roman Emperor!' the gaoler yells. 'Think you're too posh for prison, mate?'

It is 1610, in the port of Palo west of Rome. Michelangelo Merisi da Caravaggio, the greatest painter in all of Italy (as he has just informed the gaoler), has been on the run for four years. Caravaggio has lost count of the times he's been arrested. For smashing a plate of artichokes into a waiter's face, for throwing stones at the police, for carrying a sword without a licence. The only time that still causes a pang of regret is the fight he got into with Ranuccio Tomassoni. It was bad luck that no-good swindler Tomassoni pushed himself onto Caravaggio's blade. Bad luck, but they called it murder! At last the pope has granted a pardon to Caravaggio so that he can return to Rome. Only this ratbag of a gaoler won't believe him.

A fried egg. What wouldn't he give for a fried egg! Will they bring him anything at all to eat?

In his hungry thoughts, he has a vision of a table spread with a tasty meal. On the snowy tablecloth there's a basket piled with apples, grapes and pears, a roast chicken, freshly baked bread. He can smell the bread. It's maddening!

Where did he have that meal? Maybe the restaurant in La Maddalena, the artichoke place.

Then he remembers. It's the meal he put in his painting of the Supper at Emmaus. Everyone knows the Bible story. Jesus has been crucified. His followers are grieving. While two of them are walking sadly from Jerusalem to a village called Emmaus, a young man joins them. It's getting late, and they invite him to have supper with them. As the young man says the Jewish blessing over the bread, they suddenly recognise him. It can't really be Jesus, can it? He's dead. But here he is, right beside them at the table. For a moment they're too shocked to speak, and then ... he's gone.

When the nobleman Ciriaco Mattei asked Caravaggio to paint the *Supper at Emmaus*, Caravaggio did what he'd already done in several big paintings for churches in Rome. He imagined the scene as if it were happening now – in a restaurant in Rome, say. Instead of dressing people from the Bible in flowing robes, as most artists did, he painted his friends wearing their everyday clothes. Never mind if their faces were unshaven and their jackets torn. If the stories in the Bible took place today, this is how people would look.

'It's shocking! He makes Jesus's followers look like common riff-raff!' people complained.

Such attacks made Caravaggio laugh. 'What do they think a man looks like after trudging all day along a dusty road? How would they react if they saw a dead friend suddenly alive again? I've painted the Supper at Emmaus so that it feels like it really happened. You can believe in it. Isn't that the whole point?'

Caravaggio was always getting accused of making trouble. But how many people could sit patiently for as long as he could, studying the light shining through a jug of water, the black spots on an apple or the wrinkles on an old man's forehead? Sometimes Caravaggio looked so long and hard that he couldn't tell whether he was seeing or touching the things in front of him.

Suppose he painted holy scenes the way artists were expected to – as if holy people never ever burped or scratched their bottoms? He could have done that. He could have painted perfect, shiny apples, but he found them boring.

'The trouble with you,' Ciriaco Mattei once told him, after he'd paid the fine to get Caravaggio out of gaol yet again, 'is that you live in the present moment, with no thought for consequences.'

Caravaggio could have said 'thank you', but instead he said, 'Where else do you suggest I live?'

The gaoler and guard pause in their game of dice.

'Oi! Oi!' the prisoner's shouting. 'Listen to me!'

'Shuttup!' the gaoler yells back.

'Bring me some supper, and I'll let you into tricks for winning at dice. Trust me. When I've told you, you'll win every time.'

The gaoler and the guard exchange glances. The guard nods. Caravaggio presses his ear to the cell door. The footsteps and the jingling keys are getting nearer.

Saskia van Uylenburgh in Arcadian Costume
1635

31
The Flower girl
Rembrandt

His father wanted him to go to university in Leiden, so he did. But not for long. By the time Rembrandt van Rijn was 18, he was doing what he'd always dreamed of doing: training to be an artist.

Rembrandt lived in the Dutch Republic, a country that had broken away from the Catholic Church before he was born. In Italy artists like Caravaggio found plenty of work painting pictures for churches. Dutch people, on the other hand, liked their churches plain, with no distracting statues or paintings.

At home it was a different story. Art collectors covered their walls with paintings. Bible scenes, pictures of the countryside, inspiring historical events, vases of flowers and bowls of fruit. And portraits – of themselves, their children, parents and friends. Rembrandt realised that, if he wanted to earn his living as an artist, he'd better get good at portraits.

Another thing he learned was that all artists were supposed to travel to Italy. Why? Well, because Italian art was the best, wasn't it? 'We'll see about that,' thought Rembrandt. 'And anyway, why should I paint like an Italian?' He pulled faces in the mirror, trying to look dark and handsome. Hopeless! He winked at himself and stuck out his tongue.

'You think you've only got one face,' he challenged his reflection. 'Rubbish! You've got ten, twenty, a hundred. Who needs to go to Italy in search of faces?' But although he had no desire to go there, Rembrandt noticed how the greatest Italian artists, like Michelangelo and Leonardo, were known by their first names. Well then, he'd do the same, signing his paintings simply Rembrandt. Soon people stopped asking 'Rembrandt who?'

Rembrandt moved to Amsterdam, a prosperous city where his reputation grew, along with the queue of important people waiting to have their portraits painted. Like the merchant Nicolaes Ruts, who'd grown rich trading with Russia. And Dr Tulp, who lectured at the Surgeons' Guild. Rembrandt painted him dissecting a dead body while the other surgeons looked on, fascinated.

Rembrandt's portraits had something special. He seemed to capture his sitters' thoughts as their eyes lit up with amusement or clouded over with sad memories. To Rembrandt everyone's face was interesting, regardless of whether it was plain or beautiful. Even when he painted portraits of his own mother and father, he felt that every face has secret depths, no matter how well you know the person.

Smart clothes, serious expression. That's what how most people wanted their portrait to look. But it didn't have to be that way. If a customer felt like playing a role – as a soldier, say, or a Turkish prince in a turban – Rembrandt had a dressing-up box full of exotic clothes, armour, jewellery, all kinds of finery that caught his eye.

'I love this dress!' Saskia cried.

Saskia was a young relative of Hendrick van Uylenburgh, the art dealer who was helping Rembrandt to sell his work. She was his best

dresser-upper, his favourite portrait sitter. And, since June 1634 – just one year ago – she was also Rembrandt's wife. Soon, he hoped, they'd have children. These dressing-up games might have to stop then.

'I'm Cleopatra, Queen of Egypt!' Saskia announced.

'No you're not. You're Flora, the Roman goddess of Spring.'

'Oh, please, Rembrandt! I don't want to be Flora again.'

'Well, I want you to. And why not?' Rembrandt had already painted Saskia as Flora. The picture sold straight away for a good price. An ancient Roman myth plus a pretty modern face – this seemed to be a winning combination. Perhaps bit of flattery might persuade her. 'You look lovelier than the goddess herself!' he exclaimed.

Next morning, sure enough, Saskia arrived in the studio dressed as Flora.

'Stand here,' Rembrandt guided her to a place where light from the window gleamed on the golden threads in the embroidered dress. 'Don't look so serious!'

'But I'm supposed to be a goddess.'

'And I am ...' Rembrandt picked up some of leafy stems that had come with the bouquet of flowers he had bought specially in the market. He stuck them in his hair. 'I am ...' In his collar and sleeves. 'I am ...'

'Stop it! You look ridiculous!'

'All right.' Rembrandt tidied himself up. 'Calm down. There's work to be done.' Saskia's hair looked so lovely in the sunlight. He wanted to touch it.

'Just a moment.' He waved a sprig of leaves in the air. 'There – perfect!' Gently he pushed the greenery into her golden hair, as though it were an expensive ostrich feather.

'Now. Stand still.'

Saskia stifled a giggle. She'd noticed a spider on Rembrandt's collar. It must have come from the leaves. As she watched, the black thing scuttled round the back of his head.

Rembrandt flourished his paintbrush.

'Straight face. Left arm a bit lower. That's it ... and we're in business. Aargh!'

Amsterdam

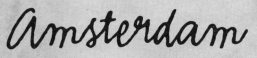

The Netherlands (1600s)

The 17th century was a Golden Age for Amsterdam. It was the most important trading centre in the world for all kinds of goods. The powerful Dutch East India Company built shipyards and warehouses. Merchants lived in grand houses along the new canals, where they displayed their art collections.

Quicker by water

Amsterdam grew rapidly. After 1625, new canals and building works were carefully planned. The canals provided a transport network and divided the city into zones, linked by bridges.

Rembrandt's church

The Oude Kerk or Old Church is Amsterdam's oldest church. Rembrandt and Saskia's four children were christened here. Titus was the only one who survived to adulthood. Saskia was buried here in 1642.

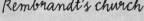

Setting sail

Merchant ships voyaged from the mouth of the River IJ all over the world, making Amsterdam a truly international city. Dutch traders established colonies in Africa, the Americas, China, India, South East Asia and Tasmania.

Workplace and home

Artists like Rembrandt worked
at home. Rembrandt had
a portrait painting studio,
a showroom for displaying
paintings for sale and a printmaking workshop, as well as
rooms for family life.

Side by side

Land was scarce, so
most houses were tall
and narrow, packed
closely together.
Merchants and
shopkeepers often
lived in the same
house where they
stored and sold
their goods.

Self-Portrait as the Allegory of Painting
1638–39

32
Painting Is Me
Artemisia Gentileschi

Cold. Damp. Narrow, filthy streets. Artemisia Gentileschi was not impressed by London. But in the royal palace near the River Thames, a log fire burned brightly in the marble fireplace.

'His Majesty will be here soon,' a servant informed her, for the fifth or sixth time that day – a winter's day in 1639. Artemisia turned to warm herself once more.

King Charles liked the paintings she had done since she arrived from Naples. He wanted to buy one for the Royal Collection. At first she was delighted, but now she felt annoyed. His Majesty was four hours late.

'You think that because I'm just an artist, you can keep me waiting,' Artemisia told the king. 'Forget it!' Only she didn't actually say the words. The argument blazed up inside her head, while she stared into the fire.

The imaginary argument became hotter and hotter, until the figure of King Charles got mixed up with the high-ranking men who used to come to her father's studio, wanting paintings. Artemisia's father, Orazio Gentileschi, was a successful artist in Naples. He painted religious scenes, full of dramatic contrasts of light and dark. 'Ah, superb! A true follower of Caravaggio!' his patrons said. Caravaggio had been dead for ten years, but his style of painting was still very fashionable.

Orazio realised that his daughter was a talented artist. As she grew up, he taught her everything he knew. Artemisia remembered how her father persuaded his patrons to order paintings from her. 'I am extremely busy at present, but if Your Lordship requires the painting soon, I humbly suggest that my daughter undertakes the work.'

'Your daughter is an *artist*?'

Yes, that's what they said. She'd curtsy and smile. The patron would stare as though Orazio had announced, 'My daughter flies to the moon on her broomstick.' But that wasn't going to stop her.

In Orazio's opinion, Artemisia's paintings sometimes took the Caravaggio thing too far – too much drama and sensation. When she painted the Bible story about Judith cutting off the head of Holofernes, she had Judith sawing through the wretched man's neck and blood spurting everywhere. Maybe she was right, though. There was quite a demand these days for violent, sensational paintings.

Artemisia became a successful artist. The cardinals, noblemen and rich lawyers who collected her paintings didn't mind when she argued with them out loud. 'Think of all the famous artists you've heard of. Now tell me – how many were women? Ten? Five? Only one? And why is that?'

After all, Artemisia reasoned, paintings were full of women. Virgin Marys, naked goddesses, great ladies in all their finery. Why shouldn't pictures be painted by women too? She had proved that they could. It hadn't been easy, but she had got there.

Some of her patrons liked a kind of painting called allegory. Allegory means 'saying things another way'. It's when an artist takes an idea like 'Truth', which you can't actually see, and turns it into a person. So 'Strength' could be shown by a picture of a weightlifter with bulging muscles. Or a woman playing the harp could represent 'Music'. The 'Art of Painting' was usually shown as a beautiful woman. There would be a second figure in the picture – the artist (a man, of course) looking on proudly.

Artemisia was determined to do things differently. Her allegory had only one figure in it – herself. 'I am the artist, and I am the Art of Painting too!'

After a few attempts, she'd worked out how to paint herself painting. She positioned mirrors so that she could see herself from the side, her hand with the brush in it reaching towards the canvas. She didn't want to look perfect. Painting can be a messy business. Her sleeves were rolled up. Her hair looked a bit wild – but what was wrong with that? 'Men think the only sort of painting we do is with makeup on our faces!' Apparently, this was the very painting King Charles wanted to buy.

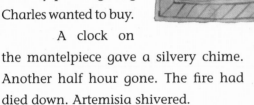

A clock on the mantelpiece gave a silvery chime. Another half hour gone. The fire had died down. Artemisia shivered.

'You English are barbarians!' she raged silently to herself. 'You keep me waiting. You can't pronounce my name. Your food is unspeakable. Your weather is appalling. You …'

Artemisia's fury was cut short by the click of a door. A little dog trotted in. It gazed at her so appealingly. She knelt down to stroke its curly head. When she looked up, there was the king.

'My dear Madam.' The king held out a hand and helped Artemisia, a little awkwardly, to her feet. 'We are honoured that you have found the time to visit us.'

'Ha!' thought Artemisia. 'Flattery will get you nowhere.' But, putting on her sweetest smile and making the smallest possible curtsy, she answered. 'The honour, Your Majesty, is all mine.'

The Maids of Honour
1656

33
Good Morning!
Diego Velázquez

'B^{oo!'} Diego Velázquez jumps. His brush leaves a black smudge on his forehead – that is, the forehead of his own portrait, which he is painting just here, to the side of his enormous painting of the royal family. He turns to see five faces looking up at him. The little princess, Margarita Teresa, with her maids of honour, Isabel and María Agustina, and their companions, the dwarfs María and Nicolas.

'Good morning, Señor Velázquez!' they sing together.

'When will our picture be finished?' little Margarita Teresa demands, staring at him with her dark eyes.

Velázquez folds his arms and stares back. 'Soon,' he promises. 'Tomorrow. *Mañana.*'

'Oh!' Margarita Teresa stamps her foot. 'You always say *mañana!*' The girls turn on their heel and run out, laughing.

Velázquez was only 24 when he painted a portrait of the Spanish king Philip the Fourth. 'From now on,' the king declared, 'only Velázquez shall paint my portrait!' For the rest of his life Velázquez was the favourite royal artist. He became the king's friend and an important courtier. King Philip gave him a big studio in the Alcázar Palace in Seville. The king was constantly dropping in to watch Velázquez at work, to admire the paintings propped against the walls, or just for a chat.

'Ah!' he'd sniff as he came down the studio steps. 'Oil paint! So,' he rubbed his hands together. 'What have you got for me today?'

In public the king never smiled. Only twice had he ever been heard to laugh. 'You'd think he was a statue,' people joked. With Velázquez, though, King Philip could relax. Still, the artist could hardly say, 'Sorry – I'm busy this morning. Could we talk another time?' Sometimes he wondered how he ever managed to finish the portraits he was always being asked to paint of the royal family and members of the court.

By 1656 Velázquez and King Philip were both middle-aged. The king seemed weighed down by worries. It upset him when the English parliament voted to cut off King Charles's head. And now Spain was at war with England, and Spanish treasure ships were constantly being attacked. 'He needs something to cheer him up,' Velázquez decided.

In his studio Velázquez set up an enormous canvas. The cloth was nailed to a framework of wooden stretchers, resting against an easel. This was how big paintings were made now, rather than on walls or wooden boards. Even the biggest canvases were light enough to move from room to room. A grand portrait of the children of the court would be a fine surprise for the king.

'Caught you at it!' The king and queen must have slipped in quietly. They were standing right behind Velázquez. The king slapped Velázquez on the shoulder. 'What masterpiece are you plotting? Come on. Let's hear.'

Velázquez had to think quickly. 'Ah, yes – it is, in fact, Your Majesty who will create this masterpiece. All I will have to do is to copy it.'

The king looked puzzled, but before he could speak there was a commotion at the far end of the studio. The princess and her friends came tumbling in, followed by their nanny, a bodyguard and a large old dog.

'If Your Majesty would care to arrange the scene in an artistic manner ...' Velázquez suggested.

'Excellent! Excellent.' King Philip bustled about, giving orders. 'Stand here, Margarita Teresa! Get into line, girls!'

At last the children settled down. Margarita Teresa stood in the centre, with her maids of honour. The dwarf María understood what Señor Velázquez wanted them to do. 'Ssh! Stoppit!' she whispered to Nicolas, who kept jumping around and teasing the dog.

'I'm in a picture! I'm in a picture!' Nicolas shouted.

'Children!' King Philip clapped his hands. 'I've got a first-rate idea. Let's play Living Statues. The last one to move gets a prize. Now. Freeeeze!'

Velázquez made quick drawings. Two minutes. Three minutes. They wouldn't stay still for long. And someone in squeaky shoes was approaching along the corridor, about to disturb them. Creak, creak, creak.

'Your Majesty,' came a man's voice. 'I do not wish to interrupt, but there is urgent news. Another galleon has been captured by the English.'

King Philip's happy expression immediately faded. He looked old and careworn.

'I'm coming. I'm coming. Velázquez, we will recommence at the same time tomorrow.'

The royal party left, in a flurry of rustling silk and clicking shoes, with the old dog shambling after. Velázquez walked over to his canvas. It was as big as the sail of a ship. That was it – it was just like setting sail, the feeling he always got, face-to-face with a new canvas. The feeling of a voyage about to begin. Exciting, but daunting too. You could never tell where it would take you. And now, in these moments when he was all alone and the studio was quiet, was the time to begin.

Landscape with Psyche outside the Palace of Cupid (The Enchanted Castle)
1664

34
Imagine Being There
Claude Lorrain

*L*ying down on the dewy grass, Psyche fell asleep. When she awoke, it was getting dark. She was in a clearing surrounded by tall trees. Among the trees a palace rose up. It was a building so strange and magnificent that it could surely not have been built by human hands. The whole palace glowed in the dusk. Psyche rose to her feet. Spellbound, she approached the doorway. Inside she glimpsed ivory ceilings held up by golden pillars. Did she dare go in …?

That's it – the bit he's been looking for. Claude closes the little book of stories. On the other side of his studio, a wide, blank canvas stands on the easel. It's time to make a start on his new painting for Prince Lorenzo.

'What should you paint for me this time? Um, let me reflect.' Claude's patron, Prince Lorenzo paced up and down. 'I know! The old Greek legend of Cupid and Psyche. A shady grove. Sunset …'

Claude was famous for his paintings of landscapes. Plenty of other artists had painted landscapes too, of course. Claude loved the deep, dreamy blues of the distant sea and mountains in paintings by Venetian artists like Titian. But no other artist knew how to fill their landscapes with airy light and shade in the way that Claude did. When you stood in front of his paintings, it was as though you could feel the sun's warmth and the cool shade of the trees.

'Do you know what is so special about your paintings?' said Prince Lorenzo. 'They make me feel as if I were there, walking in the fields and gazing at the horizon. And at the same time it seems magical, like a fairy tale.' But the prince couldn't always make up his mind. 'Maybe sunrise would be better than sunset? What do you think? Well, I leave the decision in your capable hands.'

Claude had been born in Lorraine, in eastern France, but he'd lived in Rome for most of the past 50 years. Prince Lorenzo wasn't the first to admire his paintings. King Philip of Spain had bought at least seven, and Pope Urban loved them too. Art collectors all over Europe clamoured for Claude's work.

Today in his studio he isn't thinking of them. He's thinking about when he was younger – when he used to get up while it was still dark and walk into the countryside around Rome. He'd spend all day drawing in his sketchbook. He drew quickly with his red, black and white chalks on blue paper. Trees, fields, valleys and hills, the city far away on the horizon, with its great churches and ancient ruins.

Often the only people he met were shepherds and shepherdesses taking their sheep out to pasture. When Claude turns the pages of his old sketchbooks, he can hear the jangling of sheep-bells, the nightingales singing in the undergrowth. Dawn and dusk have always been his favourite times. They both have something mysterious about them. The light grows or fades so softly, so gradually, and the trees smell green and fresh.

He'd lean against a tree trunk, drawing, not noticing how the hours passed. As the sun rose higher, shafts of light shot down through the leafy branches. The light sparkled and wavered as the branches moved. If he felt hungry, he'd dig out a pastry from his bag. When Claude first arrived in

Rome at the age of 12, he was a pastry cook. It took skill to make a really good pastry – just like a really good painting – mixing up the ingredients, keeping a light touch and a steady hand!

Today he gets out some of his old sketchbooks. Yes, here's a drawing of trees with delicate, feathery leaves that let the sunlight through. And here's one of a ruined castle, and a drawing he did in the city, of a palace belonging to one of the pope's relations. These are his ingredients. He dips a brush in thin brown paint and begins to draw with it on the canvas. Cupid's castle will stand on the edge – no, in the centre, surrounded by trees. It's a lonely place, cut off from the rest of the world … He could suggest that by putting some mountains in. These drawings of rocks will do. He can make them look bigger.

Something's missing. Something that makes you think of far-away places, of adventure, of the unknown. He remembers, when he lived in Naples for a while, how beautiful the sea was there, especially in the evening. The tiny sails of boats seemed like ghosts flying towards the sunset.

Tomorrow he'll dig out some old sketches of a shepherdess, and the one of a goddess on an ancient vase. He goes to the window and pushes the shutters wide open. The warm sun rushes in.

The Love Letter
about 1669–70

35
The Longer You Look
Johannes Vermeer

The new magnifying glass is bigger than the old one. Johannes Vermeer lifts the lens in its wooden frame and holds it at arm's length. He's fascinated by the way things look through a lens. Clearer. Stranger. He stares at a white sheet crumpled in the laundry basket that the maid has dumped in the doorway. The magnifying glass turns creases in the sheet into deep valleys. Their whiteness is like sunlight on a snowy mountain. Not that Vermeer has ever seen a real mountain. All around Delft the flat Dutch countryside stretches to the horizon.

This morning he had an idea for a painting. He was passing the doorway to the sitting room at the back of the house. He stopped in the dark lobby that was always a bit of a mess. Through the doorway the room seemed empty. The maid must have been somewhere around. She'd left her outdoor shoes on the threshold, and there was her brush. His wife's lute lay across the arms of a chair. A letter was propped on the mantelpiece. Probably another demand for payment of a bill – best ignored.

Vermeer was fascinated by mirrors too. When he turned

away from the room and looked at its reflection in a mirror, he had a funny feeling that he had never seen it properly before. He gazed in the mirror at the chequerboard pattern of black and white marble tiles. The room was like an empty stage. It was waiting for the actors to step onto it and begin their play. One would pick up the lute. Another would carry the letter – a secret letter. A love letter. A scene took shape in his imagination.

'Johannes! Johannes!' his wife called from upstairs.

'Just a moment!' he shouted.

The maid reappeared. She began sweeping, carelessly knocking the furniture with her brush. A painting of a boat at sea was hanging crooked. She pushed it straight with her finger, singing all the time.

My love he was a sailor.

He sailed upon the ocean blue.

What a shame you can't paint music, Vermeer thought. He decided to set up his easel on the landing. It wasn't the most convenient spot to paint, but he could make a start. The door frame, the lobby with its heavy hangings to keep out the winter draughts, the fireplace, the chequerboard tiles … His wife's cousin, Katrin, was coming to visit. Perhaps she would pose with the lute. And the maid might be glad of a chance to take a break from housework.

Vermeer's new magnifying glass was a present from his friend Antonie van Leeuwenhoek, who taught himself how to make lenses by shaping the glass in a fire. Last week, when Vermeer called round, Van Leeuwenhoek was in his study, staring at some kind of copper plate. 'Here,' he handed the contraption to Vermeer. 'Tell me what you see.'

Vermeer looked through a tiny hole in the plate. It had a tiny lens in it. Through the lens he saw what looked like a scrap of beautiful green lace. He looked up, puzzled.

'Beautiful, eh?' Van Leeuwenhoek nodded. 'It's only an oak leaf, but it's a leaf like you've never seen it before. My microscope reveals all kinds of things that have been there since the world began but have been invisible till now.' Van Leeuwenhoek showed Vermeer what a dead butterfly looked like through his microscope. Its wings were a cloak made from little yellow feathers. The thought of that silky colour stayed with Vermeer for days.

Like other ambitious young painters, Vermeer had begun by painting grand historical scenes. But now he prefers different subjects – a young woman reading a letter, a maid pouring milk from a jug. 'What we Dutch painters understand best,' Vermeer explained to Van Leeuwenhoek, 'is the life we see around us. Hasn't Rembrandt proved that to the world?'

'Ah, Rembrandt. What a sad loss!' Van Leeuwenhoek snapped off the butterfly's abdomen with a pair of tweezers. Only recently, in the autumn of 1669, news came of the great artist's death in Amsterdam.

The love letter scene will keep Vermeer busy for many weeks. He paints so slowly, changing things all the time until he gets them exactly right. He builds up the colours in layer after layer of oil paint. Here and there he adds pearly dots of light.

'Act like you're saying, "Is this from him?"' he'll tell Katrin, when she asks what expression she should make.

'I can't look like that for two solid hours, Johannes!' she'll complain.

When a bluebottle buzzes against the windowpane, Vermeer will think of Van Leeuwenhoek and his lenses. There are some things, he'll reflect, that become more mysterious the better you know them, the longer you look.

The House of Cards
about 1736–37

36
House of Cards
Jean-Siméon Chardin

It's a fine Sunday morning in Paris, in the spring of 1736. The Le Noir family have just returned from church. For the first time in his life, 13-year-old Louis looks forward to going to church. He can be sure he'll see Marie there. Today – no doubt about it – she actually looked at him.

'Marie, Marie, Marie,' he's saying under his breath.

'Louis! What are you muttering?' his mother glances shrewdly at him. 'Don't take your coat off, dear. You must look smart for Monsieur Chardin.'

'Mama, who is Monsieur Chardin?' Louis suspects his parents of plotting something unpleasant, like a visit from the dentist.

'Monsieur Chardin?' His father goes to the window and peers into the street. 'Monsieur Chardin is one of the most highly esteemed artists in France. He is a member of the Academy. He is …'

'Does he paint battles, or shipwrecks?' Louis asks hopefully.

'Shipwrecks!' Monsieur Le Noir looks outraged. 'Monsieur Chardin paints what we who understand painting call still life.'

'Still life?' It doesn't sound very exciting.

'A still life, Louis, is a painting of everyday objects that – ahem – as we philosophers say, do not in or of themselves possess the power of motion. Apples, for example, and jugs. And … ,' Monsieur Le Noir waves his hand as though beating an invisible egg.

'And bottles and dead fish.'

'Dead fish? Ugh!' Louis's face is a picture of disgust.

'Good morning to you all,' comes a pleasant voice from the door. 'My dear Le Noir, I see that my fame has gone before me.'

Jean-Siméon Chardin has arrived.

Is he cross? Louis can't tell. Chardin is a thick-set man with a wide face. His skin is rough and rosy, like a gardener's. He has frown lines in his forehead, dark eyebrows and a quick, intelligent smile.

Chardin accepts a glass of wine, but there's no question of settling down to pass the time of day. Louis's parents fuss around the artist. Where would Monsieur Chardin like Louis to sit? At the dining table, with the lace cloth, and the best cutlery and glasses? No? At this card table. Really? But it's only a plain little table. And the cards – Monsieur Le Noir was playing with friends last night. The cards are bent and scuffed. Let us at least get a fresh pack. No? Oh well, just as Monsieur Chardin wishes.

Chardin explains that he really doesn't want the Le Noirs to go to any trouble. Here in a hallway will be perfect, with its plain stone wall without any hangings or pictures, and the high window – not too much bright light. Perhaps Louis would like to read while Chardin does some drawings in his sketchbook?

'Or – tell me, Louis. Are you any good at making a house of cards? It takes a steady hand. A lad who can make a house of cards will grow up to be a good shot with the pistol, depend on it.'

Making a house of cards. It is the only activity Chardin has discovered that will keep a boy sitting still – still as a still life – while he draws.

'Monsieur,' Louis asks politely. 'Did you really become famous by painting a dead fish?'

'I did indeed,' Chardin nods. 'It was my *Ray-Fish* that gained me a place in the Academy.'

'Still life is the lowest form of painting.' That's what they always said at the Academy. But Chardin showed them that a still life can be painted with as much skill as a great battle. Ordinary things that we see and touch every day, like an apple or a jug, can be painted with deeper insight and stronger feelings than the figure of some legendary warrior brandishing a sword.

Now Chardin wants to prove that he can draw and paint people too. In his sketchbook he's shading the folds on Louis's sleeve, the buttons and neat buttonholes in the good, thick fabric. The boy is so absorbed in his house of cards that he's forgotten about the artist.

The stillness of people. It's even deeper than the stillness of things, Chardin thinks. Why has that blush appeared on the boy's cheek? What – or rather who – is he thinking about?

Chardin smiles quietly. None of my business. He starts to draw the cards. He'll do a few more drawings before he begins the painting, back in his studio. Last night, how many times those cards passed from hand to hand. What hopes were pinned to the little pictures of knaves, kings and queens!

Le Noir amuses Chardin with his 'objects that do not possess the power of motion'. Onions, copper pots, bowls of fruit, playing cards. Chardin loves these ordinary, silent things. He knows that it is the artist – and only the true artist – who has the power to make them speak.

Revolution!

1750—1860

Scientists weighed, measured and experimented in an attempt to find out exactly how the world works. Poets and writers were more concerned with things that can't be weighed and measured, like love, freedom, justice and genius. Artists too were stirred by such ideas. And whether they wanted to or not, they couldn't help being swept up in the great events that took place at this time, from the French Revolution of 1789 to the Napoleonic Wars that raged across Europe for much of the next 25 years.

By the time Napoleon was defeated at the Battle of Waterloo in 1815, another revolution was changing the face of Europe. Steam-powered engines, factories producing goods that were shipped around the world, and rapidly growing cities – this was the Industrial Revolution. Incredible fortunes were made by factory owners, but for workers times were often hard. Many emigrated by steamship to North America, where railways were opening up the entire continent to white settlers. People began to travel more and to experience the art and culture of other countries. Woodblock prints by Japanese artists such as Katsushika Hokusai started crazes for Japanese art in Europe and America in the nineteenth century.

Artists looked at a world changing before their eyes. Was their task now to champion the new or to celebrate the traditional? Both seemed important in this age of revolutions.

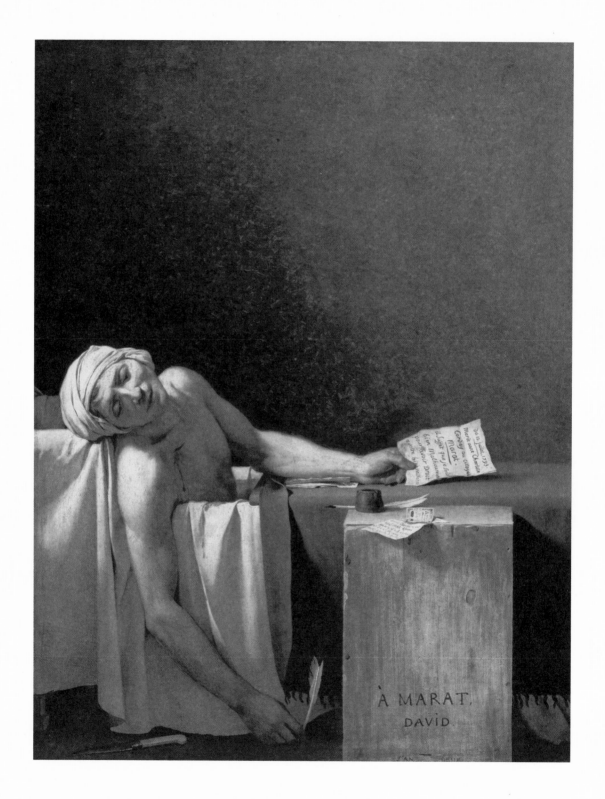

The Death of Marat
1793

37

The Storm and the Calm

Jacques-Louis David

'Citizen David! Citizen David!'

Who's that yelling up from the street? There's always somebody shouting. What do they want this time? Jacques-Louis David's face frowns back at him from the mirror. His dark eyes look even fiercer than in the self-portrait on his drawing board.

David puts down the board and wipes the ink off his pen. He'll finish the drawing later.

'Citizen David!' It's Robespierre's secretary. 'I have a note for you. It's urgent!' Robespierre is David's friend. He's one of the most powerful men in the revolution that has swept King Louis off the throne of France. When Robespierre speaks, you listen.

'Bring it up then,' David shouts down. He pulls the window shut.

David was born here, in Paris. It was never a peaceful city, but these days as soon as you step into the street you feel violence boiling under the surface, ready to break out. If anyone can control Paris, it is Robespierre. He has a will of iron.

In January, crowds gathered in Revolution Square to watch King Louis go to the guillotine. The king had been plotting to bring a foreign army into France to put him back on the throne. 'The traitor must die!' decreed Robespierre. David remembers how the crowd fell silent a moment before the terrible blade came swishing down. The king's head fell into the waiting basket . . . whump! The crowd cheered.

Long live the revolution!

For too long the kings of France let their subjects struggle and starve while they feasted in their palaces, along with the nobles. That will never happen again. Now the people are in charge. And Robespierre and his fellow leaders of the revolution will see that it stays that way. In the old days, kings and nobles paid artists to make them look powerful, and the artists obeyed. That too is finished. David wants to serve the revolution. A painter must tell the truth!

Robespierre's secretary is at the door, red-faced, panting from running up the stairs. He gives David the note. It's about Jean-Paul Marat – a man David knows well. He can't believe his eyes. Marat is *dead*? The secretary nods. David catches his sly stare, watching to see how he reacts to the news. He turns away.

It's only a couple of days since David last visited Marat at his house. He was busy writing, as always. His writings inspire brave and noble actions for the good of the people. The note explains that Marat has been murdered. It seems that the young woman who killed him, Charlotte Corday, is already in prison. Why did she do this? Could she have thought that a single thrust of a kitchen knife would change the revolution's course?

It's not long before David receives another note, from the revolutionary government, asking him to paint a picture of Marat. It will hang in the council chamber and inspire the leaders of the

people. Of course he will do this. How better can an artist serve the revolution? The people must know what has happened. No one must ever forget.

He goes to the church where Marat's body is lying before he is buried. Outside it's a summer's day. Inside the building, the damp, greenish light is like the pale skin of the dead man's face. Marat looks peaceful. What was he thinking the moment Charlotte Corday lunged at him with her knife? He'd been writing in his bath. He often did this, because the warm water with oatmeal in it soothed his eczema.

David thinks of the pictures he once painted of heroic scenes from ancient stories. That was what was expected of artists when he was young, before the revolution. You could paint a dramatic moment, full of passion and high ideals, but everyone in it had to be wearing historic clothes.

His picture of Marat will be different. It will show the death of a modern hero. Should he paint Charlotte Corday wielding her knife while Marat helplessly raises his hands to defend himself? No, he will paint the moment just afterwards, when Marat is breathing his last. A man slumped over in an ordinary bathtub, the pen still in his hand, the fresh wound in his chest. This friend of the people hasn't been writing on a shiny, expensive desk but on an old wooden box.

When David starts to paint Marat's face, he imagines that he is listening to Marat talk, as he used to. 'I have been thinking, my friend, about how, straight after the execution of the king, the streets of Paris felt so peaceful, and the people were so calm.'

David will paint just such a moment. The unreal calm after something has happened that you never dreamed you would live to see. The moment when you realise that life will never be the same again.

The 3rd of May 1808 (Execution of the Defenders of Madrid)
1814

38
No Heroes
Francisco Goya

Jean-Paul Marat died in 1793. Throughout Europe kings and nobles anxiously followed the news from France. Would it be their turn next? The French Revolution was a monster devouring everything in its path. In 1794 they heard that Robespierre himself had been guillotined, and the artist Jacques-Louis David imprisoned. Then in 1799 a young army officer called Napoleon Bonaparte took control of the government.

In Spain the court painter Francisco Goya was secretly excited by the French Revolution. His country, too, cried out for a new beginning. Meanwhile he painted portraits of King Charles and his courtiers. Take away their silk clothes and powdered wigs, and they were the same as anyone else, really, with their hidden thoughts and odd habits.

King Charles of Spain was more interested in hunting than politics. 'The French Revolution will burn itself out,' his advisers said. Bang! The king fired his shotgun. Another partridge fell to the ground. Goya portrayed the king standing proudly in his hunting clothes, with his dog gazing up at him.

Back in France, Napoleon's power grew. In 1804 he had himself crowned emperor. Jacques-Louis David was back in favour. Goya heard that he'd painted an enormous picture of Napoleon's coronation. Everywhere people were talking about the new emperor. He had started as a humble soldier. Now, at the head of a great army, he had defeated the Italians, Austrians and Russians. Napoleon didn't have time to take potshots at partridges.

In November 1807 Napoleon's army entered Spain. It was supposed to be a friendly army. 'We'll invade Portugal together, and divide up the spoils,' the French generals promised. But it wasn't long before Napoleon forced King Charles off the throne and made his own brother, Joseph, King of Spain. This was not the revolution Goya had hoped for.

The people of Madrid weren't very fond of King Charles, but they didn't want a French king instead. On a May morning in 1808, thousands of Madrid's citizens attacked the French soldiers who had just marched into the city. The fighting lasted all day. By nightfall the soldiers were winning. They rounded up everyone they could find and set about taking revenge. Before dawn, firing squads were at work, executing Spanish fighters and unarmed bystanders alike. Groups of captives shuffled through the streets – labourers, doctors, teachers and priests, men and women. They did not know whether they would live or die. For the next five years, Spain was plunged into war.

All this time, Goya was hardly able to paint. Who wants their portrait painted in the middle of a war? Instead he made drawings of the terrible sights he witnessed and the horrors he heard about. Villagers chased out of their homes by soldiers, dead bodies lying by the road, starving and wounded people with nobody to help them.

At last the French army was defeated and forced to retreat from Spain. A new government was formed. Goya went to them with a suggestion. 'I want to paint what happened in Madrid, at the beginning of the war.'

He knew about David's painting of the death of Marat, but he didn't want to paint a picture about heroes. 'I have not seen many heroes in this war,' Goya reflected. 'I have seen violence, suffering, helplessness. It is not heroic. It is meaningless.' Of course the government might want a painting that showed the Spanish people as heroes and the French soldiers as villains. But it seemed to Goya that it was not so clear-cut. Who can tell what good or bad things any person is capable of, especially in war?

On a dark night, you're usually glad to see a lighted lamp. But that night the soldiers carried big lamps so that they could see to shoot. And the people they shot did not know what was going on. There was a workman who was trying to get home, with his pickaxe over his shoulder. The soldiers said he was carrying a weapon. 'What do you mean?' He'd raised his hands, and the lamp lit up his old work shirt.

Goya stared at his paintbrush. It was his favourite brush. He'd managed to hang onto it all through the war. Once he had used it to paint the frothy gold braid on King Charles's waistcoat. 'Very clever, y'know. The way you get that delicious shiny effect,' the king was impressed.

Clever. What was the point in cleverness?

Perhaps the man's wife had washed his shirt the day before. He'd have enjoyed putting on a fresh shirt that morning. When it was dark and he still hadn't come home, she'd have been afraid. Was the man a hero? Was he just in the wrong place at the wrong time? Goya could not decide. The white paint glistened on the tip of his brush.

The Wayfarer above a Sea of Fog
about 1818

39
Rocks and Stones and Trees
Caspar David Friedrich

'Of course. Choose whichever one you want!' Caspar David Friedrich smiles. It's the fourth or fifth time this week that his neighbour's young daughter Else has knocked at his studio door. Each time she has the same request.

'Please, sir. May I look at the scratches?'

'Sketches,' he corrects her. She likes the sketches with animals or birds in them. He always lets her pick one to take home. Yesterday she chose a drawing with a spider's web. All she can find this morning is a pile of rocks with a stunted tree and a miserable old crow perched in its branches. Her face lights up.

Children understand life better than we do, thinks Friedrich when she's gone. They see things with their own eyes. They haven't yet been taught what to like and what not to like. What does Else do with his sketches? Perhaps she invents stories for them. 'Once upon a time, there was a wise old crow …'

He returns to the painting on his easel – a man standing

on the summit of a mountain, looking into the distance. The idea came to him in a dream. As soon as he woke up, he made a small drawing in the notebook he keeps beside the bed. He has copied the picture onto a canvas, very lightly, in ink. He has made it bigger, and it will change in other ways too as he works on it. But it is still the picture he saw in his dream. 'You must see a painting in your soul before you can see it with your eyes,' he tells his friends.

Friedrich's studio is a bare room in a house on the edge of Dresden. Bare wooden floor, bare walls, window, chair, easel. That's it, except for the sketches spread out on the floor. He did most of these on a walking trip in the mountains east of Dresden. They'll be useful for his new painting, reminding him of the exact shapes of the sandstone peaks and rocky slopes. Yes, he can see the landscape clearly, the rocks worn into fantastic shapes by wind and rain. One looked just like a bear. Another resembled the side of a man's face, with the nose and chin jutting out.

The figure he's painting is himself, exactly as he appeared in the dream. He was wearing his best velvet coat, not his old walking clothes. But he wasn't at a party or a wedding. He was alone in the mountains. Friedrich uses a very fine brush to paint his hair, blowing slightly in the breeze. He feels as if he has stepped outside himself. What is the figure thinking as he stares into the distance? Friedrich should know. And yet ... and yet he can't put those thoughts into words. It's like trying to reach out and touch the horizon!

One time when Friedrich was walking in the mountains with Franz, his old schoolfriend and hiking companion, they spent the night at an inn. When they woke, grey fog pressed at the windows. They could see nothing. They set off anyway, along the forest path that led up and up to the mountain. Cold fog clung to the branches. The only sound was the snapping of twigs underfoot. At last they emerged into open, stony ground. Fog rolled around them, sometimes thicker, sometimes thinning away, as though the sun were trying to break through. Then, all at once, they walked out of the fog into clear air. For a moment, neither of them spoke.

'It feels like we're kings of all the world!' Franz said at last.

'I don't feel like a king.' Friedrich was thoughtful. 'I feel as though we are the only men alive. There is only us and …' he looked around. As far as they could see, rocky outcrops rose through the fog. In the furthest distance grey mountains merged with the pale sky. 'And the Soul of Nature.'

'Hmm,' Franz knelt down, rummaging in his rucksack. 'Don't tell me we forgot the bread and cheese. I'm starving!'

Friedrich remembers that morning, stepping out of the fog and into the sunlight. He felt that he was seeing the world for the first time, through fresh eyes. It's easier to feel that way on a mountain than here in his studio, to be sure. Where's the drawing he made of those rocks that look like a man's face? He can't find it anywhere. Ah! Else must have taken it.

'Tell me,' he says the next time Else pops her head round the door. 'What do you do with my sketches? Are you making a little book of stories?'

'Oh no, sir!' The thought has obviously never occurred to her. 'I use them to wrap up my toys!'

The Great Wave off Kanagawa,
from the series Thirty-Six Views of Mount Fuji
1831

40
Under the Wave
Katsushika Hokusai

You like that picture – where the big wave is about to come crashing down on the boat? Yes, everybody loves that one. I'll bet you don't know who the artist is, though. Guess. No, it's not Hiroshige, definitely not. You want to guess again? All right, I'll tell you. It's my grandfather.

When I say that my grandfather is one of the most famous artists in Japan, people ask if they would have heard of him. That's a difficult one! He's changed his name more than 20 times. See. On the side of the picture it says 'By Hokusai, who changed his name to Iitsu'.

You've heard of Katsushika Hokusai. Of course you have. It may seem crazy, but Grandpa believes that, because an artist's work changes as he grows older, his name should change too. He told me that he was five years old when he started to sketch and that he didn't do any really good paintings before he was 70! Can you believe it? 'When I am 110 every line I draw will be alive,' he says. 'If *you're* still alive,' we say. 'Even your brushes will need walking sticks by then!'

He likes a good laugh, but there are some things he's very serious about. He's obsessed by Mount Fuji. I admit that it must be the most beautiful mountain in the whole world. It's as though an artist had dreamed it up, with its curved sides and covering of snow. Grandpa can't stop drawing and painting it. This picture of the great wave, with Fuji in the distance, was the first of his *Thirty-Six Views of Mount Fuji*. Now he has started *A Hundred Views of Mount Fuji*!

The *Great Wave* is my favourite of all his pictures. I was with him when he took the painting to be made into a print. We went to the printmaking workshop, where the *horishi*, who carves the woodblocks, had a lovely smooth block of cherry wood ready. He pasted the painting onto it. Then he began to carve, following the lines in Grandpa's picture. He carved along even the thinnest, most delicate lines. He would have to carve a separate block for every colour in the picture – dark blue, lighter blue, brown, even the soft, cloudy grey of the sky.

Some time later I accompanied Grandpa again, this time to watch the *surishi*, who does the printing. He applied coloured ink to the woodblocks. He laid a sheet of paper on top of each block in turn and rubbed it hard so that the ink stuck to it. Grandpa watched carefully. One tiny mistake and the print would be spoiled!

The *surishi* printed lots of prints of the *Great Wave*, and they all sold. That dark blue colour was something new. It's called Prussian blue. You can buy it from the Dutch merchants in Nagasaki. Perhaps it was talking to the merchants that made Grandpa think about being out at sea. I have a little fishing boat of my own, so I know what it's really like.

Those boats in the *Great Wave* are taking the fishermen's catch to market in the city of Edo as fast as they can. They do this every day. But at sea you can quickly get into trouble. You must keep an eye on the waves, make sure you don't get caught underneath one as it breaks. It happened to me once. I was knocked overboard and forced down and down by the weight of water. My lungs were bursting. 'If I try to breathe, I'll drown,' I thought. But somehow, at the very last moment, I was back at the surface.

Wouldn't I like to forget that experience? In a way. But I still love the sea. I love watching waves break. And in this picture my grandfather has caught the wave at the very moment it topples over. It's terrifying, exciting and beautiful. I feel as if I am in the water myself, looking up at the face of the great wave.

If you're interested, I'll show you some more of Grandpa's work. I've got these books he made to teach people how to draw. Look – he used the same little figures and drew them in different poses. *Manga* he called them. And here's another print of Mount Fuji, and another one, *Fuji in the Snow*. Is he a rich man now? Unfortunately not. People's tastes in art change all the time – like an artist's name, hey? People want prints by Hiroshige now. I've got some of his too.

Sit down. You'll share a cup of rice wine with me? I'll introduce you to Grandpa one of these days. Here's a toast to him. A toast to … no, Iitsu doesn't sound quite right. To Hokusai. May he live for ever!

The Open Door
Fourth version, April 1844

41
Artistic Chemistry
William Henry Fox Talbot

'Damn! Damn and blast and ...'

William Henry Fox Talbot gave his wife a strained smile. 'I'm sorry, my dear. I'm just having a fit of complete and utter creative despair.'

His drawing of the lake was rubbish! The water looked like porridge. The trees were hairbrushes stood on end. He had hoped that the clever little gadget he'd brought with him would help. It had mirrors that reflected the view as well as the paper you were drawing on. All you had to do was trace the image onto the paper – supposedly! But his drawing was nothing like the view. It had clearly been drawn by someone who couldn't draw to save his life.

But what if ... What if he could capture an image, the way a mirror captures a reflection? What if he coated a sheet of paper with a chemical that reacts to light? Talbot was always having brilliant ideas. At university he studied ancient literature, but he was incredibly good at maths and chemistry too. Back at Lacock Abbey, his ancient family home in the country near Bath, he began experimenting.

Everyone knows that some materials react to light. 'Look, Constance,' he lifted up a lamp that stood on his desk by the window.

'Look at what?' asked his wife. Under the lamp was a perfect circle of dark, shiny wood, while the desk around it had faded to a dry, sandy colour.

'The light has drawn a circle.'

'Perhaps it's time we bought a new desk?'

Talbot knew that a chemical called silver nitrate is extremely sensitive to light. He brushed silver nitrate onto a sheet of paper. Then he laid a big, flat leaf on top and put the paper in bright sunlight. Half an hour later, he lifted up the leaf. Underneath, like magic, was its shape on the paper. The sunlight had blackened the paper around it, but it couldn't shine through the leaf so easily. Where the leaf had been, its pale shape was left on the paper, perfect in every detail.

'What do you think?' he showed the picture to Constance.

'You've improved a great deal, I must say.'

'Oh no, my dear. I didn't draw this.'

'Then who did?' They had no guests staying in the house, as far as she knew.

'We have an artist among us!'

'An artist? I wasn't aware that anyone had arrived. Pray tell me who he is.'

'His name is Mr Light! This drawing was made by Light alone, without anybody's help!'

Constance stared at the picture of the leaf. It showed all the delicate detail of the branching veins. It was beautiful. She had never seen anything like it.

Talbot was onto something. He put a sheet of specially coated paper inside a box with a single tiny hole in one side for the light to get in. Then he stood the box in front of a tall window.

Like a leaf, the window had many sections, with dividing lines between them. Sunlight shone through the window into the hole in the box and onto the paper he had put inside.

When he took the paper out, there was a picture of the window. Only it was inside out, with dark shapes where the light streamed in and pale shapes where the window frame blocked the light. After more experiments, Talbot worked out how to turn the inside-out picture into a picture that looked exactly like the actual window, only in black and white. There was one problem. Because it took time for sunlight to act on the chemicals, he could not make pictures of anything that moved.

But was that such a problem? He loved the paintings of Vermeer and other Dutch artists of the seventeenth century. Vermeer's house must have been full of movement – he had 11 children! – but in his paintings everything felt still. A jug on the table, a picture on the wall. And every object was painted with the same attention. 'A painter's eye will often be arrested where ordinary people see nothing remarkable,' thought Talbot.

He walked around his big old house, into the stable yard. The farm hands were harnessing horses to the wagon. The scent of new grass drifted from the meadows. He stopped by a stable door. Someone had left a broom lying on the path. He picked it up and propped it against the wall. The strong sunlight cast sharp shadows. It was the kind of scene that most people would think too ordinary to be worth recording. Vermeer, though – he'd have understood its charm. Talbot began to feel excited. He could picture the new masterpiece that would soon be drawn by the pencil of Light.

Snow Storm – Steam-Boat off a Harbour's Mouth
1842

42
I'll Show You!
Joseph Mallord William Turner

Even in the harbour, alongside the jetty, the water surged and fell with the storm swell. The sides of the steamboat grated against the harbour wall. 'Take care, sir!' the mate called to an old man who was about to step aboard. 'Take care yourself,' the old man answered gruffly, grabbing hold of a rope. He jumped onto the deck with an awkward thump. He pulled his oilskin coat straight on his shoulders and with both hands jammed his hat down on his head.

'Do your worst!' he shouted at the heavy grey clouds overhead.

He took a deep breath. Salt spray, seaweed, fish, tar. The age-old smell of the harbourside. And coal smoke. Greasy, black coal smoke, mixed with hot steam. That was a new smell since he was a boy, 60-odd years ago. You smelled it everywhere today. By the sea, in cities, in open fields where railway lines had started to run out from the towns in all directions.

J. M. W. Turner – Professor Turner of the Royal Academy in London – was a great painter, most people agreed. His new paintings weren't easy to get the hang of, though. It used to be different, in the days when he painted scenes so you could tell what was what – a church in a valley, say, or a seashore with fishing boats. Turner was famous for the way he painted atmosphere. He could capture the effect of the morning sun shining through mist, the hazy air of a warm summer evening. The trouble was, Turner's new paintings seemed to be nothing *but* atmosphere, with hardly any recognisable shapes in them.

The mate glanced at the old man, who'd sat himself down on a coil of rope. 'I'd go below, sir, if I was you. It'll be rough when we get into open water.'

As the steamboat chugged out into the North Sea, along the coast of Essex, the swell became bigger and bigger. Up went the little boat as a wave rolled under it, then down, down into the trough, where walls of grey water loomed above. The wind rose. A spattering of freezing sleet thickened into a snowstorm.

Professor Turner of the Royal Academy sat on the coiled rope, staring. Staring at what? the mate wondered. In the thick snow flurries, there was surely nothing to see. Luckily it was only a short voyage, along the coast to the next harbour.

When he was a young man, Turner painted scenery in a theatre. He'd always loved the play by William Shakespeare called *The Tempest*, in which the magician Prospero calls up a terrible storm at sea. It wrecks the ship carrying his enemies. Only, because it is a magic storm, no one is hurt. Driven by the wind, the sleety snow stung Turner's face and stirred up his imagination. He would paint this storm. The salt spray, the snow, the steam, and the little boat wallowing between the waves. It would be a picture of two astonishing forces meeting head-to-head – the power of nature and the power of the steamboat engine, chugging through the storm as though nothing could stop it.

When Turner showed his painting of the steamboat in the storm at the Royal Academy in 1842, people couldn't work it out. 'Is that dark lump in the middle meant to be a boat? They say Turner's a genius, so why doesn't he paint things properly? You can't tell which of those white patches are waves and which are sky.'

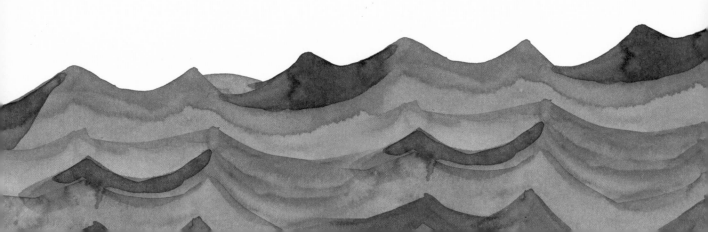

'It's nothing but soapsuds and whitewash!' someone exclaimed.

'Soapsuds and whitewash!' growled Turner when a friend told him about this comment. 'I wonder what they think the sea's like? I wish they'd been in it!'

Turner liked to tell the dramatic tale of his steamboat trip. '"Lash me to the mast," I ordered the crew. "I want to experience the storm in all its might." At first they wouldn't listen to me, but at last they agreed. I promise you, I didn't expect to come out alive.' Each time he told this story, the storm became stormier and waves wilder.

'Turner's certainly a genius,' people started to whisper. 'But he's just – you know – a little bit mad.'

Turner guessed what they were saying. What did he care? At his house by the River Thames, in the village of Chelsea, he could live quietly. He sketched the boats, on their way to and from London. At the Royal Academy there was talk of some chap called Talbot. He had invented a new science of drawing with light. What did he call it? Photogummy-something? It would never catch on.

This evening the sun hung red in a clear, cold sky. Turner walked down to the river. Suddenly he felt angry.

'Soapsuds and whitewash!' he shouted into the frosty air. 'I'll show you!'

His breath came out in puffs of steam.

London
England (early 1800s)

In the early 19th century, the Industrial Revolution transformed Britain. During Turner's lifetime, London more than doubled in size. The village of Chelsea by the River Thames, where Turner lived for about 18 years, was absorbed into London.

go faster!

Around 1797 Turner drew Old Battersea Bridge, the last wooden bridge across the Thames. In 1844 he painted a steam train crossing the river. Life was speeding up!

Sails to steam

The Industrial Revolution was powered by steam technology. Stagecoaches were replaced by steam trains and sailing boats by steamboats.

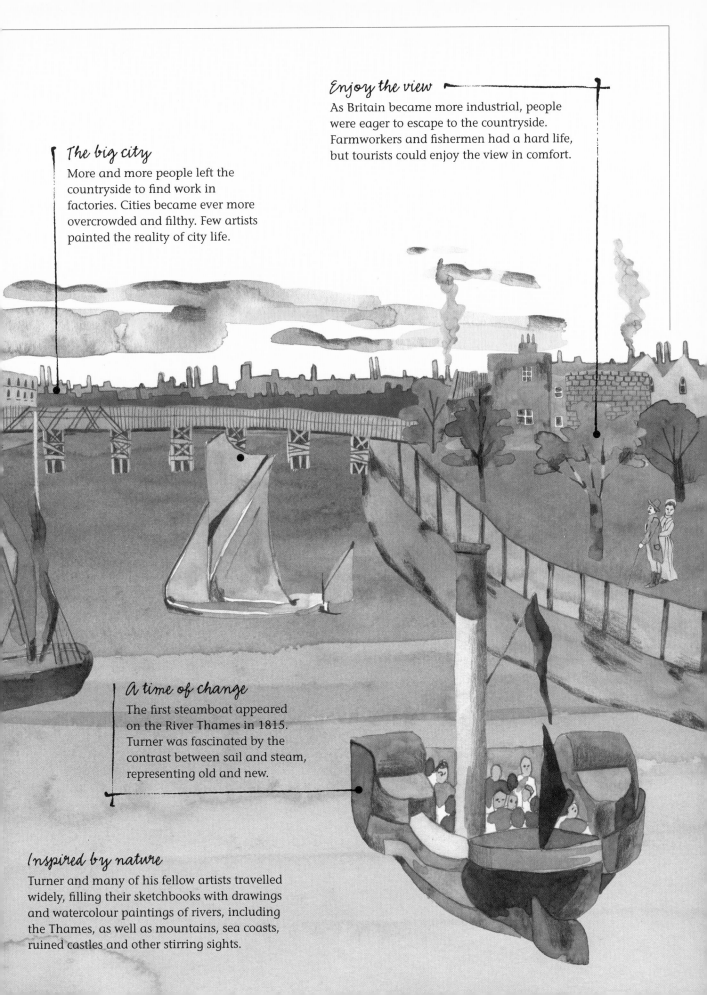

The big city

More and more people left the countryside to find work in factories. Cities became ever more overcrowded and filthy. Few artists painted the reality of city life.

Enjoy the view

As Britain became more industrial, people were eager to escape to the countryside. Farmworkers and fishermen had a hard life, but tourists could enjoy the view in comfort.

A time of change

The first steamboat appeared on the River Thames in 1815. Turner was fascinated by the contrast between sail and steam, representing old and new.

Inspired by nature

Turner and many of his fellow artists travelled widely, filling their sketchbooks with drawings and watercolour paintings of rivers, including the Thames, as well as mountains, sea coasts, ruined castles and other stirring sights.

The Meeting
1854

43

The Plan of Campaign

Gustave Courbet

The shadows of trees across the dusty road begin to shrink. The blue of the sky becomes lighter, harder. At the start of a hot day Gustave Courbet can feel the heat radiating from the fields beside the road. He has been trying to find the right words for what he wants to say to Alfred Bruyas, turning them over in his mind.

I want my paintings to be about the times we live in. No, that's not quite it. How about *I want to paint people as they really are*? Maybe. He kicks a stone, watching it roll into the dry grass. *I want to create a living art. That is my aim!*

'Good morning!' Courbet calls to an old man who passes him, leading a donkey. The man just nods. He and the donkey are on their way to market in the nearby city of Montpellier in the south of France. They both look exhausted.

Courbet hurries on, his thick, black beard bristling with excitement. They have so much to discuss, he and his new friend Alfred Bruyas. His Rich New Friend, who happens to be an enthusiastic collector of art. Together they are going to astonish the French public. They will change people's ideas about art for ever.

This is their plan – well, Courbet's plan, which Bruyas seems pretty keen to support. They will hire a large marquee and set it up in the centre of Paris. Inside the marquee Courbet will show his paintings.

Bruyas can display his own art collection, which already includes some terrific paintings by Courbet. A perfect combination!

Courbet's eyes glitter with a triumphant, mischievous light. He can almost hear the kinds of things that well-off Parisians will say about his paintings of peasants and workers. 'Oh, how perfectly horrid!' they'll exclaim. 'Look at that man's ugly red face! When we come to an art gallery, we want to see beautiful pictures. We don't want to look at paintings of rough, lower-class people. Ugh!'

Can that be Bruyas in the distance, coming towards him? Courbet strides on, swinging his walking stick. He has to admit that he enjoys it when snobbish city folk are shocked by his paintings. Though why should they be shocked, after all? 'I just paint the plain truth,' he thinks. 'Hardworking peasants can't primp themselves up with face-powder and hair-curlers. Real people have flabby tummies and fat bottoms. They don't look like Greek gods made from porcelain.'

Hah! These spoiled Parisians will be even more shocked when they find out what's coming. Courbet and his friends believe that, through their art and their writings, they are preparing the way for a better and fairer world. In this world, farm and factory workers will be properly rewarded. On the other hand, the fashionable people who spend their days swanning around in shops and cafés and – oh, all right, yes – art galleries too … Well, they'll realise that they are not nearly as important as they imagine. Courbet and Bruyas, the farmer's son and the banker's son, will stand in the front line of this revolution, like soldiers who race ahead to be the first to engage the enemy. Yes!

'Or,' thinks Courbet, 'you could see it like this. I, the artist, am like a craftsman who travels from town to town, using his skills to improve the world. I work hard, but I'm a free man. I have no master telling me what to do.' In his next painting, he decides, he'll portray himself as just such a craftsman, carrying his painting kit on his back along this dusty road. He'll paint Bruyas greeting him – the meeting of two great minds! Bruyas will be well-dressed, thoughtful, eager to hear about Courbet's new ideas. His servant will be there too, a bit awkward in his best clothes but just as much part of the picture as they are.

He will paint the picture quickly, as he usually does. Maybe he can finish it and show it to Bruyas this week.

'A living art!' Courbet brandishes his stick, as though rushing into battle.

Two girls walking to market, arm-in-arm, giggle at the crazy artist. 'Mesdemoiselles!' Courbet plucks off his hat and bows. 'I hope to paint your portraits one fine day!'

The girls gawp at him and quickly walk on.

'You will become living art!' he calls after them.

The marquee might cost – what? Fifty thousand francs? If he could persuade Bruyas to provide, say, thirty thousand … Hmm. Courbet does quick calculations in his head. If he sold most of his paintings, they could end up with a good profit. He'll shock the socks off those Parisians. But the strange thing is, they go away shocked, and then – would you believe it – they come straight back for more …

Niagara
1857

44
Worth Every Cent
Frederic Edwin Church

The line of people stretches around an entire block in Lower Broadway, inching forward. New York swelters in the fine May weather. Every time a carriage passes it churns up a little dust storm, making people cough.

We're all waiting patiently for the chance to see Frederic Edwin Church's new painting, *Niagara*, which is on display in a gallery along the street. Mr Church is young, but already he's one of the most famous artists in America. He has travelled far and wide, painting our American landscape – incredible, inspiring scenes of mountains, rivers, places you can only dream of visiting. At this moment in the spring of 1857, I've decided that, one day, I'm going to be an artist too. Of course I've seen pictures of Mr Church's paintings in a magazine, but this will be the very first time I get to see one in real life.

On the wall a poster announces that, for the privilege and pleasure of viewing Mr Church's *Niagara*, there is a charge of 25 cents per person. In front of me there's a boy waiting with his parents. He pinches his mother's arm. 'Seventy-five cents! You could buy a box of soldiers for that!'

'It will be worth every cent, young fellow,' his father says sternly. 'Mr Church is a hero. He's travelled to the Andes Mountains. He's fought his way through forests and jungles, I dare say, with nothing but a sketchbook to defend him from bears and snakes. His paintings make me feel proud to be American. Over in Europe they have their ancient cathedrals, but Mr Church has proved that our great wonders of nature are every bit as awe-inspiring.'

While the father is giving his son this lecture, I notice a man beside me looking quietly amused. He has bushy side-whiskers and a floppy necktie. I feel sure I've seen him before. Then it dawns on me. It was *him* – in the photo in the magazine. I studied that photo carefully, because I need to know everything there is to know about being an artist – what artists wear, what they look like. 'You're Mr Church, aren't you, sir?' I whisper. The man presses a finger to his lips and winks, so I'll keep the secret.

When we get inside the crowded gallery, Mr Church goes to the back of the room. I make sure I'm standing beside him. 'You know,' he says to me, but like he's talking to himself,

'every day when I'm in New York I go to my studio. Just me and my paintings all day long. So this morning I thought, "Let's find out how my painting gets by when it's out in the world on its own".'

Over people's heads I can see *Niagara*. Every detail is sharp as a photograph, yet the painting is big – so much bigger than any photograph – and the colours are luminous, like there's a light shining through them from underneath. The water streaming over the edge of the falls – sparkling white, glassy green – makes the stuffy room feel cool and fresh. The rainbow-rosy mist feels so airy. I can't figure out how Mr Church did this. It's more real than real.

I pluck up courage. 'What was it like at Niagara Falls, sir?' I ask.

'Indescribable!' he says. 'Imagine, the water thunders so loud you can't hear yourself think. The great moving curtains of the waterfall – they make you feel this big!' He holds up his hand so thumb and forefinger almost meet. 'The spray flies up in clouds and soaks your clothes. It was one of the most uplifting experiences of my life. It was …,' he shakes his head. 'It was like being in the presence of God!'

In my mind, the rumbling of carriage wheels outside is mixed up with the deep, booming voice of the falls and the gigantic force of the moving water. While I was waiting, I'd been impatient. But now it's the opposite. I lose all track of time. I look around at the other visitors – the men and women with serious, lit-up faces, like people's faces in chapel.

Much later, I set off on my own travels. 'If you want to be an artist,' people kept saying, 'go to Paris.' So that's where I headed. I couldn't believe that none of the artists I met there seemed to have heard of Frederic Edwin Church. And I realised that the things I'd admired so much about *Niagara* – its grandeur, its astonishing, luminous detail, its noble vision of nature – all those things were considered kind of old-fashioned by young artists in Paris. I'm ashamed to say that I stopped singing Church's praises. But let me tell you, I've never been so completely swept away by a painting as I was by my first sight of *Niagara* that day.

Seeing It Differently

1860–1900

Of all the machines developed during the Industrial Revolution, the camera made the biggest difference to artists. For the first time since the cave painters, here was a new method of capturing the way things looked. And when it came to detail, the camera only took a second to do what might take an artist days or weeks to finish – an eyelash, an earring, a blade of grass. When Van Eyck or Dürer had painted these details, people were amazed by their skill. Now every photographer could do the same.

But early photographs couldn't capture vivid colours or the atmosphere of a summer's afternoon by a river. Painting found a new direction. Rather than recording the appearance of things, artists wanted to recreate what people felt while they were looking at them. A painting could be more than a picture of something else, like a vase of flowers. It could be an experience all of its own, a different experience that came from the paint itself – all the dabs and strokes of colour, the textures and shapes.

Artists wanted to make the experience of looking so exciting, so full, strange and beautiful, that people would see the world around them with fresh eyes. Painters experimented with all kinds of brushstrokes and different ways of combining colours. Sculptors worked in traditional materials like stone and clay to create their new visions of the human form.

The Cradle
1872

45
Cradle of Art
Berthe Morisot

'Which paintings should I put in the exhibition?' Berthe Morisot wanted to know what her sister thought. Edma would have a better idea than anyone. She could easily have become an artist herself. It was such a pity she never picked up her paints and brushes now.

The exhibition that Berthe and other young artists were planning in April 1874 would be utterly different from the official exhibition called the Salon, which took place in Paris most years. As everyone knew, the Salon jury only accepted certain kinds of paintings. 'Boring paintings for fatheads,' was how Berthe's friend Edouard Manet put it. He used ruder words for the artists who were favourites with the jury.

'I'm not sure I approve of that Monsieur Manet.' Berthe and Edma's mother liked young men to be polite and amusing. Above all they must not 'stir things up'. Madame Morisot was always inviting polite young men to dinner in the hope that one of them would marry Berthe. After Edma got married, Berthe was expected to do the same. And already Edma had two adorable children!

What was wrong? Berthe was so pretty. Only she should stop frowning so much while she painted. In Madame Morisot's opinion, men preferred wives who were not too serious. Or too artistic. 'Art is all very well,' she liked to say. 'But compared to the joys of motherhood, it's no future for a well-brought-up young woman.'

Edma was sure that, whatever Mama thought, Berthe was right to go on painting. She had so much talent. Monsieur Corot, the sisters' last teacher, had seen that Berthe was a real artist, a serious artist. How quickly she'd learned from him to paint with those light, feathery brushstrokes. How definite she was about the subjects she wanted to paint – the places she and Edma visited together, their family and friends.

Berthe's paintings made you feel as if you were enjoying the same things she enjoyed. Going out for a picnic, sitting reading in the shade, watching children playing hide and seek. They were about moments when you feel happy to be alive, when life flows of its own accord and carries you along.

'You know my favourite painting,' Edma smiled. 'It's the one of Blanche in her cradle.'

Edma's little daughter Blanche was two years old. Yet it hardly seemed a minute since Berthe painted her as a tiny baby, sleeping contentedly while Edma looked on. That day her sister was wearing a beautiful silk jacket, ready to go out to visit friends. The carriage was waiting by the porch. But Edma couldn't tear herself away from the cradle. She wasn't anxious about leaving Blanche. Not at all. It was just that she couldn't stop looking, as if she could not bear to miss a single breath, the smallest movement of the baby's sleeping face.

Manet admired Berthe's painting. 'I like the way you've painted your sister and the baby differently,' he said. 'Edma's portrait is fully formed, while the baby's is sketchy. It's like new life, so delicate. And Edma's hand, touching the cradle – it seems as if even her fingers are lost in thought! You know,' he laughed, 'it's good to see a portrait of a beautiful woman who isn't thinking the slightest bit about herself.'

'Oh, not like me, you mean?' Berthe didn't mind being teased. Manet had recently painted Berthe herself, wearing a dashing black dress and holding a posy of violets. Unlike the portrait of Edma, Berthe's dark eyes gazed straight out of the painting. 'I predict,' said Manet, 'that you will soon have the art world at your feet.'

Around the time Berthe painted *The Cradle*, an art dealer called Paul Durand-Ruel asked if he could display her paintings in his gallery. She couldn't believe the prices he proposed to charge. They were higher than the prices that other artists in the gallery – who were all men – were getting for their work. 'See?' she told her mother. 'You were wrong.' Madame Morisot had a habit of saying that Berthe's painting was a nice hobby, but it would never make any money.

Berthe and the other artists who were now planning to exhibit their work together had a lot in common. They wanted to capture the atmosphere of a scene, not to record all the minute details of people's clothes and faces. If details were what you wanted, why not take a photograph instead? Like Berthe, they wanted their paintings to create the impression of a passing moment, full of life, where sunlight stirred up the colours and the air seemed to move.

'You think I should show *The Cradle*, then?' Berthe pressed her sister.

'I predict,' Edma did her funny imitation of Manet's voice, 'that you will soon – '

'Stop it!' Berthe exclaimed, blushing.

Saint-Lazare Station
1877

46
The Great Outdoors
Claude Monet

'Now you've heard about me,' said Berthe Morisot, 'I want to tell you about my friend Claude Monet. Today, of course, everyone's heard of Monet. And I must say, he was always very determined to make an impact. One morning in 1877, for example, Monet marched into the stationmaster's office at Saint-Lazare railway station. He'd put on his best suit and was brandishing a gold-headed walking-stick. Such confidence! The poor stationmaster was bowled over. Monet persuaded him to order the trains to come and go, puffing out great clouds of smoke and steam, so that he could paint the scene. Imagine – at one of the busiest stations in Paris!

'Even if Monet was exaggerating, I can't help thinking of that story when I see his paintings of Saint-Lazare. He worked like mad, painting 11 pictures. In this one, I love the way he's captured the smoke drifting gently into the high roof, and the sky and tall buildings in the background – so calm outside the hubbub of the station. See how he's picked out the gleam of the rails, the glint of steel and glass, with those quick brushstrokes. It's one thing to paint outdoors by a quiet riverbank, but Monet had to prove he could do the same thing in a railway station. A true painter of modern life – a true Impressionist!

'What's an Impressionist? I'll explain. When a group of us put on our first exhibition in April 1874 – me, Monet and 28 other artists – a lot of people sneered at our work. But a few understood what we were doing and why our exhibition looked totally different from the official Salon. Our paintings didn't tell stories. We didn't fill them with highly polished details. Instead, we wanted to paint the real feeling of looking – the sensation of a single moment when shapes, colours and movements, shadow and light, all come together in one impression. *Impression, Sunrise* – that was the title Monet gave his painting of the port of Le Havre on a misty morning, with the red sun reflected in the water. Art critics started to call us all "Impressionists", and the name stuck.

'There was another difference between us and the Salon artists. They might go out sketching, then come back to their studios to paint their pictures, but we often painted out-of-doors. Monet's painting of Saint-Lazare Station wouldn't have been the same if he'd been remembering what it was like rather than painting right there, in the midst of it all. In fact, no one was more fanatical about painting out-of-doors than Monet. He would probably claim that it was he who struck the first blow for Impressionism – or rather, dug the first hole!

'Here's another story. Back in 1866, when Monet was an unknown young artist, his wife looked out of the window one day to see him digging a trench in the garden. "What on earth are you doing?" she called. "Can't you guess?" he shouted. "I'm starting a painting."

'No artist had ever done what Monet was about to do – paint an enormous painting entirely out-of-doors. His huge canvas went into the trench. He fixed up a pulley to raise and lower it, so that he could paint every part without climbing a ladder. He painted four women in the garden, wearing fashionable summer dresses. He was convinced this picture would astonish the Salon jury – after all, they loved big paintings full of figures. But the jury couldn't make head or tail of *Women in the Garden*. They expected big paintings to show an inspiring historical scene. "Rejected!" they said.

'Some artists would have given up. Not Monet. As a teenager growing up in Le Havre he'd been taught by Eugène Boudin, an artist who painted outdoors in the brilliant seaside light. For Monet, this was what art was all about. In 1870 he painted his wife with Madame Boudin on the beach. "How careless! He's got grains of sand in the paint!" That was the kind of reaction he usually got.

'Today it's the opposite. Monet is one of the most famous and successful artists in France. He's bought a lovely house in the country, at Giverny, near the River Seine north-west of Paris, and he's just bought some land next door with a little stream. Monet has plans for a water garden, with a pond and a Japanese bridge. I can imagine him, staring for hours at the reflections in the water, at the upside-down sky and the trailing branches of willow trees. I can see him painting the lily-pads, like green clouds – floating in the moment, like the clouds of smoke in Saint-Lazare. That's his dream garden. But I imagine Monet's going to be spending as much time with his spade as with his paintbrush for some time to come!'

Paris

France (late 1800s)

In 1888 Paris was preparing for the World's Fair, where French achievements and culture would be proudly displayed for international visitors. France was not the most powerful industrial nation in Europe, but Paris was the leading centre for new ideas in art, design and fashion.

Time off

The Tuileries Gardens in front of the Louvre provide a large, elegant public park. They were a popular place to meet and relax – and for artists to observe the world go by.

Grand designs

The Eiffel Tower was designed by Gustave Eiffel as the entrance arch for the 1889 World's Fair. At first artists objected that it would spoil Paris, but it soon featured in their paintings.

Eiffel Tower

Follow the river

The River Seine flows through Paris towards Argenteuil, Giverny and other places where Impressionist artists worked. Their paintings often show riverside scenes.

Artists' quarter

Many artists, including Monet and Van Gogh, lived and worked in the district of Montmartre, where rents were cheap. They met at cafés and cabarets like Le Chat Noir, or Black Cat.

Le Chat Noir

Look and learn

The old royal palace of the Louvre housed an enormous art collection that was open to the public. Artists came here to study and to make copies of great works of art.

uileries ardens

Louvre

The Horse in Motion
1878

47

Split-Second Timing

Eadweard Muybridge

'Whoa there! Steady, now. Steady!' The jockey is having trouble calming Sallie down. What's making the mare so jittery? As the jockey pulls her head round her hooves dance on the spot. Anything could set her off.

It's the photographer, Mr Muybridge. He talks too loud. His stupendous beard waggles like a bear in a bush. He waves his arms. And he's got a pistol in one hand. Sallie doesn't like guns. Or beards for that matter.

'Mr Moobridge, sir. I think you could be making the horse nervous. She's all ready to go, sir, when you are.'

'Muybridge,' the photographer flourishes his pistol. '*Edward My-Bridge*. If you please!'

Eadweard Muybridge strides off towards the racetrack where Mr Stanford is waiting. Six years ago, in 1872, Mr Stanford had photographs taken of his horse Occident trotting. Special photographs that only Muybridge knew how to take. He made a camera so its shutter worked much faster than other cameras. He could photograph a trotting horse, and the photo came out sharp and clear, not all blurry.

What Leland Stanford – one-time governor of California, railway tycoon, art collector and racehorse owner – wanted to find out was this. When a horse is trotting, is there a moment when all of its feet are off the ground? He reckoned there was, but nobody had been able to prove or disprove this. The human eye couldn't grasp that split second. But Muybridge's camera could.

His first photograph of Occident trotting was a sensation. It proved that not one single painter or sculptor in the whole of history had got it right. The way they'd shown horses in motion might be splendid, but the positions of the legs were all wrong. Without exception.

Stanford felt that he'd backed the right man. He'd had a hunch that Muybridge, an eccentric English photographer with a reputation for violent outbursts, would work out a way to answer his question. Stanford had admired his photographs of the natural wonders of Yosemite Valley. Not so long ago, the only way most people could see such wonders was in grand oil paintings by artists like Thomas Cole and Frederic Edwin Church. Now all you had to do was buy an album of Muybridge's photographs.

It takes a big man like Leland Stanford to deal with Muybridge, though. The photographer was in a stagecoach accident in Texas some years back. He fell out of the stagecoach and cracked his head on a stone. That could be what makes him say and do crazy things. You don't want to get too near him when that pistol's swinging from his hand.

The jockey sees Stanford and Muybridge waiting together by a line of 24 cameras on the side of the racetrack. Each camera has a tripwire attached, stretching from side to side of the track. This time Muybridge has made the shutters so they work at two-thousandths of a second. When Sallie gallops past the cameras, her legs will trigger the shutters. Click, click, click – all 24 of them. There'll be 24 photographs of the different movements made by the galloping horse.

Muybridge lifts one arm. Crack! With the pistol shot, Sallie is off. By the time she reaches the cameras, she's hurtling along. The tripwires don't bother her. In the blink of an eye she's through the other side. Stanford has got what he wanted. The photographs demonstrate exactly how the legs of a galloping horse move, with sometimes just one, sometimes no hooves touching the ground. Who can have dreamed it was possible to take action photographs like this?

From now on Muybridge becomes unstoppable. He photographs people – walking, skipping, jumping, playing leapfrog, every movement you can imagine and some you can't. He photographs a bird in flight. Its wings looks nothing like the wings of birds in paintings. It proves that you can't tell the whole story with a single picture. When someone asks, 'What does a galloping horse look like?' you need many pictures to answer that question.

If Muybridge hadn't had that stagecoach accident, maybe he would never have had these brilliant ideas. Who knows? He soon has another idea. Muybridge puts pictures of a galloping horse around the edge of a circular glass plate. The plate slots into a machine that shines a beam of light through it while it turns. The light projects the pictures onto a screen. Across the screen gallops a shadowy horse, the world's first moving image.

What should Muybridge call his projector? 'A Magnificent Machine for Looking at Living Things in Motion'? Not very catchy. 'Zoopraxiscope' sounds more scientific. He turns the little handle and the glass plate whirs round. The oil lamp inside the projector shoots out its yellow beam. In a patch of light on the wall, the black ghost of a horse gallops like the wind.

A Sunday on the Island of La Grande Jatte
1884–86

48

What Is Colour Made Of?

Georges Seurat

After the first Impressionist exhibition was held in 1874, it became a regular event, attracting lots of visitors. In April 1879 the fourth Impressionist exhibition opened in Paris. Among the young students eager to see what they could learn from these artists was 19-year-old Georges Seurat. He was studying painting at the School of Fine Arts. He was fed up with the way his old-fashioned tutors made him spend day after day drawing dusty old statues. He loved the Impressionists' open-air scenes dancing with colour. You could feel the sun's warmth and the air alive with light.

'This is more like it!' His eyes shone. 'It makes me want to go home and start painting straight away.'

Before Seurat could really become an artist, however, he had to do military service in the French army. He carried a notebook everywhere, sketching the soldiers and his surroundings in the seaport of Brest. He didn't have a chance to paint, but he read about theories of art, especially about colour.

A year later Seurat was back in Paris. Now he could get down to work. Above all, he wanted to put his ideas about colour into practice. Was there any such thing as 'pure' colour, he wondered? Red, say – if you put a red shirt next to something blue and then next to something green, the exact shade of the red seemed to change, although of course it was still the same shirt.

Seurat was excited by the Impressionists, but did they really understand what colour was made of? He studied what scientists had written on this subject. You can't just say 'the grass is green', he decided. In reality the grass is lots of colours – brilliant white reflections; purple, blue and black shadows; brown and orangey dry bits; as well as fresh green leaves, with yellow, white or pink flowers hiding among them. It's our eyes and our brains that bring all these colours together into a sensation that we call 'green grass'. Seurat began to look at everything in this unusual way.

Some of Seurat's friends thought his theories were getting too complicated. 'You can't make a painting by sticking your nose in books,' they objected. But in 1884 he exhibited a painting that took everyone by surprise. It was two metres tall and three metres long. It showed a group of men and boys sunbathing on the banks of the River Seine and splashing about in the water. Just the kind of scene the Impressionists liked, you might think.

Seurat's painting was different, though. He had painted it using a completely new method he'd worked out for himself.

Instead of mixing different colours, then brushing the mixed paint onto the canvas, he painted thousands of little spots, lines and patches of unmixed colour – green, pink, white and blue – all next to each other. And it worked! If you went close, you could see all the individual dabs of colour. When you stood further away, the colours merged into the impression of a warm, grassy riverbank, of the blue summer sky seen through a heat haze.

Seurat was already at work on another enormous painting. He'd decided to paint a typical Sunday afternoon on an island in the Seine called La Grande Jatte. This time he was even stricter about using the tiniest dots of bright colour. He combined innumerable colour dots to make the figures of elegant ladies and gentlemen relaxing in the shade of trees, a girl in a red dress skipping, a rowing boat, a monkey on a lead. So much was going on in this big, still, mysterious painting.

Seurat was proud of his new method of painting. He called it 'chromo-luminarism', which was a bit of a mouthful. Soon people were calling it 'pointillism', from the French word for a dot, *point*. Seurat moved on to painting circus scenes and seascapes, but already some of his fellow artists were getting tired of the shimmering effect of all those dots.

'That's how our eyes really see colour,' Seurat asserted.

'Maybe you're right,' they said. 'But to *our* eyes your way of painting things makes them look a bit unreal.' Seurat got cross. He fell out with some of the Impressionist painters, whom he had once admired so much.

Then, in September 1891, Seurat died suddenly from an unexplained illness. It could have been pneumonia or a heart attack. No one was sure. He was only 31, yet he was the leading artist of a new type of art. After Seurat's death, no other painter carried on with his total dedication to pointillism. All the same, his invention got artists thinking. 'A picture is a collection of colours. Red, green, blue, yellow. These are the keys of our piano, the strings of our guitar. Let's see what new tunes we can make them play!'

The Starry Night
1889

49
Vincent's Starry Night
Vincent van Gogh

There's a tap at his door. The nurse's voice: 'Time for bed, Mr Van Gogh.' 'One moment,' he calls. 'I'm just finishing a letter to my brother.' The nurse's footsteps go away.

In another room a patient is yelling and thumping the wall. The mental hospital can be a noisy place, and Vincent van Gogh needs peace. Peace! But at least he has his painting to get on with. And the nurses and doctors are kind. They encourage him to paint. Van Gogh feels that painting is the one thing that will keep him sane.

He puts down his pen. He's so sleepy! Today he woke before it was light. He got out of bed and went to the window. There was the great shadowy cypress tree, the moon riding high and the sky still full of stars. The wind blew from the mountains. The cypress bent in the strong wind, reared up, bent over again as if alive. Thin clouds chased across the sky. What was to stop him going up there, among the stars? As he looked up, Van Gogh felt closer to the stars than to the wooden floorboards of his bedroom. He felt closer to the past than to the present. Down below, was that the little church from his old home in the Netherlands? No – impossible. This was France. This was now. The stars swirled in his head like thoughts.

'What a mess I've made of my life,' Van Gogh reflects. 'I'm 36 years old, living in a mental hospital, painting pictures nobody wants. One mess after another.'

His very first job had been working for an art dealer, until he got fired. Then he became a preacher and gave away all his belongings to poor people. He got fired again. Then finally, just a few years ago, it dawned on him – he was destined to be an artist!

He worried he'd never be any good. There was so much to learn. But the best place to learn was definitely Paris. He must go there! To begin with Van Gogh had painted with browns, greys and dull greens, as if the sun never shone and nobody felt happy. In Paris he realised he couldn't go on like this. The Impressionists' vivid colours lifted his spirit. And Seurat – Van Gogh loved his paintings. Colours aroused feelings, so – maybe – if he arranged colours in a certain way, he could give people certain feelings. Joy, calm, hope … He studied Seurat's method carefully.

The excitement of Paris was overwhelming – meeting artists, discovering new kinds of art, working hard, hanging out in cafés. Van Gogh dreamed of success, but when he looked in the mirror, a scruffy, penniless artist stared back. Paris was not working out. He must move on.

Van Gogh was enthralled by the Japanese prints he'd seen in shops and galleries. Japanese artists like Hokusai depicted everyday scenes in rich, deep colours. If only he could travel to Japan! But he was much too poor. The next best place, Van Gogh decided, was the far south of France. In February 1888 he took the train to Arles.

Spring came, then summer. Around the ancient town, almond orchards blossomed. All day Van Gogh drew and painted in the countryside. He worked quickly, not with tiny dabs of colour like Seurat

but much more impulsively. That was how he felt about the fields of sunflowers, with their strong, tall stems and flaming yellow heads. Not patient but unbelievably excited! When you were face-to-face with a sunflower, its intense yellowness was … Ah! He couldn't find the words, but he could try to paint it.

Sometimes Van Gogh missed the company of fellow painters. He invited Paul Gauguin, another penniless artist he'd met in Paris, to join him. He got the spare bedroom ready, hanging his sunflower paintings around the walls to greet Gauguin with a fanfare of yellow. And then? The two artists would work side by side, spurring each other on.

For a while things went well. But Gauguin was a proud, difficult man – not the best sort of friend for Van Gogh. They began to argue bitterly. One winter night, after a particularly violent quarrel, Van Gogh was so upset he sliced off part of his left ear. 'I'm getting out of here!' thought Gauguin, and packed his bags. Alone again, Van Gogh became scared of what he might do next. To be safe, he got himself admitted to a mental hospital. Yes, it was for the best. The doctors would keep an eye on him …

Van Gogh feels too tired to finish writing his letter. He was trying to describe what he felt this morning, under the stars. But words can't describe it. No – tomorrow he must paint it. He will paint the starry night.

The Wave
1897–1903

50
In Her Hands
Camille Claudel

What do I do? I'm an art critic. 'Who needs critics?' you might say. 'We're all free to make up our own minds about art.' Of course – and that's fine by me. So long as you don't make up your mind to think the same as everybody else!

Take our great French public. Today, in 1898, we are obviously a nation of art-lovers. Otherwise why would so many thousands of us visit the Salon each year? And who does everyone agree is the greatest sculptor in France? Why, Auguste Rodin of course. Rodin, Rodin, Rodin. That's the name you hear, because that's the name everyone repeats.

I don't deny it. Rodin is a great sculptor. But you know what? I sometimes ask people, 'Tell me why Rodin is such a genius.' And they will say, 'Look at that statue's hands. They're so expressive. Only Rodin can make the human hand speak like that.'

'Aha!' I'll say. 'Do you know who sculpted those hands? It wasn't Rodin himself. It was Camille Claudel.' They'll stare at me in disbelief, because they obviously haven't heard of Claudel. Or if they have, they don't realise what a brilliant sculptor she is, and just how much Rodin owes her.

I know Claudel quite well, and I'm convinced that one day she'll have the fame she deserves. As a young girl she was already making sculptures out of clay, soil, anything. When she was 16 she persuaded her parents to let her study in Paris. She shared a studio with some other girls. Then their teacher left, and it was Rodin who took his place. He saw at once that Claudel had talent – a lot more talent and determination than he was expecting in someone so young. Anyhow, to cut a long story short, Rodin was working on a big project for the government, a huge monument with dozens of figures. He invited Claudel to become his assistant.

She continued to make her own sculptures. 'What a promising young artist,' people said. 'But you can see how she's influenced by Rodin.' What they couldn't see was how Rodin was being influenced by her. They couldn't believe that an unknown young woman was giving ideas to this famous French sculptor. I can't help thinking that, if Camille Claudel had been a man, it might have been a different story.

Claudel loved Rodin, but it upset her that people thought she owed everything to him. You know how Rodin's figures are always naked, Michelangelo-style? Claudel started sculpting figures with clothes, so they'd look as different as possible from his. She went away and stayed with a friend of hers in London for months on end. Rodin was heartbroken, I'm told. But he still wouldn't come clean and say, 'I owe a lot to Camille Claudel.'

Why do I think so highly of Claudel? Her sculptures express a person's inner emotions. You forget that you're looking at a block of marble or a lump of bronze. It's as though you feel real sympathy with the sculpture. She made a piece with two dancing figures. You can feel the love that's drawing them together, the rhythm of the music that makes them want to dance. Yet it's only a small sculpture, like a lot of her work. Small, but full of movement and emotion.

The last time I visited Claudel in her studio, she was carving a lump of onyx marble. It was a little sculpture of a wave, curling up in one powerful movement, just about to break and come crashing down. 'Do you know Hokusai's *Great Wave*?' I asked. 'Who doesn't!' she laughed. And even if she'd been thinking about Hokusai's picture, her great wave was very different. She'd made a plaster model, which showed how the sculpture would look when it was finished. There were three young women, playing or dancing under the crest of the wave.

It seemed to protect them and at the same time to be something wild and dangerous. I could sense how they were enjoying this carefree moment together. The wave made them crouch in anticipation, excited and frightened at the same time.

Claudel talked to me about how the beautiful watery green of the stone would contrast with the figures of the girls, which would be cast in bronze. The figures looked so lively, so delicate – nothing at all like Rodin's figures.

'In my opinion, Camille,' I said, 'you're a genius.'

She gave a wry smile, as if she thought I was trying to flatter her. If I'd said the same thing to Rodin, I shouldn't think he'd have doubted me for one second.

Anyway, I hope that I've persuaded you to look again at the work of Camille Claudel. Are there any other artists I would recommend? Ah yes, you really must go to see Monet's new water-lily paintings.

Sainte-Victoire Mountain with Large Pine
about 1887

51

It All Fits Together

Paul Cézanne

Dear Monsieur Bernard, perhaps you will understand …

Understand what? Paul Cézanne put down his pen. He was trying to reply to the enthusiastic letter he'd received from Emile Bernard. This young artist, it seemed, was an ardent fan. 'Master', he addressed Cézanne. Master! No one had ever called him that before. He sighed and rubbed his beard. How could he explain his way of painting to this young man? It had taken him a lifetime to work it out, and he was still not satisfied with the results …

Cézanne was an expert in being misunderstood. In the early days of the Impressionist exhibitions, where he had shown some of his first paintings, his fellow artists thought his work looked clumsy. Not so long ago, the writer Emile Zola – his old schoolfriend – had based a character in a novel on him. Zola could not deny it! The miserable failed artist in his novel was based on himself, Paul Cézanne. Everyone could see that. 'What a shame Cézanne turned out to be a failure,' they said behind his back. 'He was 56 before he had a proper exhibition!'

But now, suddenly, young artists were interested in his work. They wanted to do something different from the Impressionists, different too from Van Gogh and Gauguin. In their search for a new kind of art, they turned to him. Oh, he wished he were not getting old. How amazing it must be, at this time in history, with so much happening in the world of art, to be young, to have everything ahead of you …

For an artist, who lives through his eyes, it can be hard to put things into words. Cézanne wrote some more words, but they did not express what he felt. He crumpled the letter up and started again.

The artist's true path is the study of nature. Go to an art gallery and study the great artists of the past, but then … But then you must go outside and study the forms of nature …

How many times had he walked out of Aix, the beautiful city of fountains and leafy alleys, into the countryside? He thought of his special place, where he could look across the valley of the River Arc to Sainte-Victoire Mountain. There was enough shade under the pine trees to paint through the day.

He remembered one day in particular, it must be 15 years ago or more. He'd set up his easel. Thirteen kilometres away, the mountain

seemed to lean towards him across the distance. Baking in the sun, its rocky sides were grey, brown, blue. The colours swam through the trembling air. He painted little patches of colour, the brushstrokes going all one way – across, up, down – there and there. He built up the picture out of colour patches as if he were building something solid – like the mountain, silent and solid and far away. Lightly, quickly, he added dark lines for the edges of fields, houses, the top of the viaduct that carried steam trains in and out of Aix. A hot breeze blew, stirring the scent of the pine trees and the wild thyme that grew among the rocks. If he moved his head to the left, the branches of the pine tree followed the outline of Sainte-Victoire Mountain. He painted them, short strokes of black, a touch of red, of blue. The pine tree and the mountain knew nothing of each other, but they both belonged in his painting.

Monet would have painted the shimmering colours of sunlight dancing among the pine branches. A feast for the eyes! But there was more to nature than colours and light. There was a logic to nature, a structure, like building blocks. Cézanne painted a tiny patch of red on the roof of a farm building. He could not explain it in words, but when he was painting, he felt how the different parts of nature fitted together. He could almost *understand* …

How could he explain to Bernard the structure of nature, the way the mountain and the valley and fields all related to each other, like different notes in harmony? Cézanne had tried to stop caring what people said about him. 'A failure! A recluse, hidden away among country bumpkins in the South of France.' He *did* care what Bernard thought, however, and the other young artists who claimed to admire his work so much. *Think of nature in terms of three-dimensional forms, like cones and spheres …*

No! No! Bernard would think he was mad. He ripped up the second letter. There was only one solution. Bernard must come to visit. They would walk together to the special place. They would stand in front of nature. And nature – as only nature can – would talk to them.

War and Peace

1900–1950

When artists, or scientists or any other group of people get together in one place, sharing discoveries, comparing ideas, competing to be the best – that's when things happen fast. Paris was one of these places.

In Paris around 1900, people began to expect that every artist who wanted to make their mark would do something so mind-bendingly new that at first it was shocking. Like the Cubists, with their baffling broken-up pictures and constructions, or, a bit later, the Surrealists, with their weird dream paintings and sculptures glued together from odds and ends.

But, however shocking art could be, nothing was as shocking as being caught up in a war. Between the start of the First World War in 1914 and the end of the Second World War in 1945, many millions of people were killed and many more millions displaced, their lives changed beyond recognition.

Artists all over the world responded to these cataclysmic events in many different ways. In Russia, artists joined with designers, architects and engineers to make art part of everyday life, wanting their work to serve a new and better kind of society. Other artists believed that art should provide something beautiful and reassuring, while yet others took scraps and broken fragments from the war-torn world around them and turned them into art.

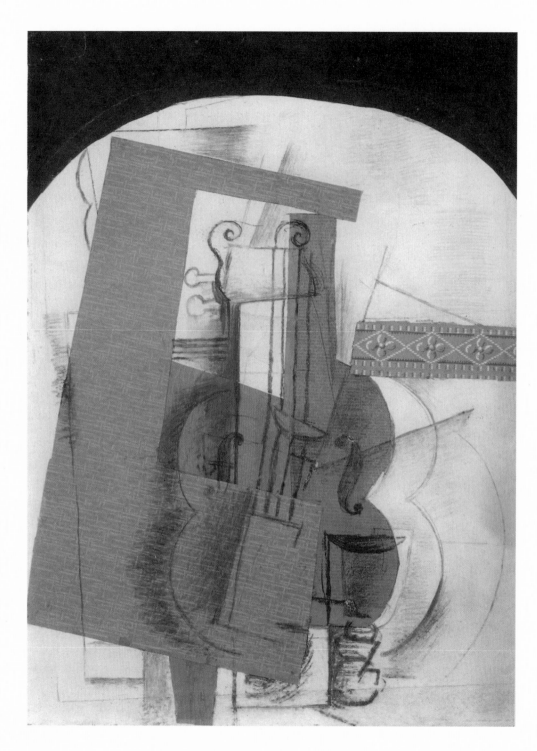

The Violin
early 1914

52
Cut and Paste
Georges Braque

Sketchbook. Socks. Toothbrush. Had he forgotten anything? Ah, yes – Cézanne! The photograph of Cézanne's painting of Sainte-Victoire Mountain was creased and thumb-smudged. It had holes from being pinned to studio walls. Now it would accompany Georges Braque on his latest, most dangerous adventure. He was off to war.

He tucked the photo into his suitcase and shut the lock. He looked round his studio, for the last time perhaps. Stacked against the walls, his paintings stared back at him. Above them hung more paintings and curious objects that Braque had collected in markets and junkshops – musical instruments, African masks. On the table was one of the many collages he'd made this year. By cutting out pieces of wallpaper, sticking them down and adding details with a stick of charcoal, he had made a picture of a violin. It was very satisfying to bring together different shapes and lines, like fragments of something broken, and turn them into something new.

Beside the violin picture lay scraps of newspaper and wallpaper he'd cut out, ready to start another collage. Braque hesitated. Maybe he could take these bits and pieces with him to the army barracks?

'*Soldat* Braque!' he imagined an officer yelling. 'This is war! It's time for you *artistes* to get real!'

In August 1914 Europe was suddenly at war. Braque was going to join the French army. His Spanish friend Pablo Picasso would stay behind in Paris. They had often joked that they were like outlaws in the Wild West, fearless adventurers breaking the rules of art. 'Get real!' Braque smiled to himself. Wasn't that exactly what he and Picasso had been trying to do for the last six or seven years?

In their paintings and collages they used real newspapers and wallpaper. Picasso even used a piece of rope and some cloth patterned to look like a chair seat. Throughout history, artists had tried to convince people that objects in a painting were really there – apples that looked good enough to eat, portraits you half expected to speak. You pretended that a picture was a window into another world behind the frame. When you thought about it, though, the only thing that was *really* real about a picture was the picture itself – the canvas and paint, or the pieces of paper and traces of charcoal and pencil that it was made of. Everything else was in the imagination of the artist making it or the person looking at it. Braque and Picasso felt that they were the first artists to see this clearly.

What did it mean, anyway, to see an object or a person? Humans aren't like cameras – one blink and there's a picture. When you look at an ordinary jug, for example, you see the curve of the handle. Then you notice light gleaming on the side. Shut one eye, move your head, and the jug changes shape. You find yourself staring at the tabletop or a lamp. A single picture brings together many separate moments of looking.

Cézanne understood about these many moments of looking. After he died in 1906 there was a big exhibition of his paintings in Paris. It was there that Braque first realised that he didn't want to paint pretend-window pictures any more.

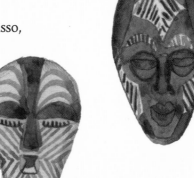

It was around this time that he met Picasso, a young artist who had moved to Paris from Barcelona and was quickly making a name for himself. Most artists settle into one particular way of painting. Picasso could paint brilliantly in any way he chose. When Braque went to Picasso's studio he was working on a weird painting of five naked women. Some had faces like African masks or ancient carvings. The table and curtains were broken up into angular shapes, like smashed glass. Picasso noticed that, unlike other visitors, Braque's mouth did not drop open in sheer incomprehension.

For the next few years, Braque and Picasso were like 'two mountaineers roped together', as Picasso said. They painted completely new kinds of paintings and made lots of collages. Their pictures were like strange, angular jigsaws of shapes and lines, with clues in them, like a fragment of a guitar or a moustache or a wine bottle. They weren't like looking through a window. They were like walking into a room full of mirrors – thousands of moments of looking, all happening at once.

'You're not seriously saying that's a work of art? How is that a picture of a violin?' They heard plenty of comments like that. At the same time, art critics in Paris enjoyed inventing new names for new kinds of art. 'Cubism' was the name they gave Braque and Picasso's paintings and collages. 'OK,' the artists were too busy working to give it much thought. 'If you want to call our art Cubism, go ahead.'

Braque glanced at his watch. The train to the barracks left in half an hour. The German army had invaded Belgium. France would be next. On second thoughts he opened his case again and slipped the scraps of paper in.

Birthday
1915

53
Happy Birthday!
Marc Chagall

Four whole years! It was four years since Marc Chagall and Bella Rosenfeld last saw each other. Now Chagall was back home in Vitebsk, painting, painting all the time. 'I never see you without your paintbox!' Bella laughed.

In 1910 Chagall left Russia and travelled to Paris. He rented a studio. He visited galleries, where he saw paintings by Courbet, Manet and many other artists. So much was happening in Paris! There were the Cubists, whose pictures were like watching a magician juggle with broken-up shapes. The *Fauves*, or 'wild beasts', who painted a woman's face bright green or a tree trunk flaming red. He saw poets and musicians, singers in street cafés, aeroplanes like flying bookshelves in the sky. 'In Paris, I found everything,' he told Bella.

In the old Russian Empire it was difficult for a young Jewish artist to travel. The Imperial authorities didn't usually allow Jewish people to leave the towns and villages where they were permitted to live. Chagall had been lucky. He went on being lucky. He'd just exhibited 40 paintings and lots of drawings in a gallery in Berlin. People were starting to notice his work. 'Chagall's art is unique!' they said.

'They're right,' Chagall grinned, seizing his hat and striding out into the summer evening. 'I have to admit that I am a pretty unique artist.'

'You're a pretty unique bighead, if you ask me, Marc Chagall!' Bella teased him.

What if he was? Bella still loved him. And he loved her. She was even more beautiful than he remembered. In Paris Chagall had painted with intense, rich colours, filling the world around him with an atmosphere of magic and dreams. A cat with a human face miaowing at the Eiffel Tower, a steam train running past upside-down. Men and women floating above buildings. Roofs and walls, earth and sky, animals and people seemed to break apart and slide together like pictures in a kaleidoscope. In Vitebsk he painted portraits of Bella and himself. *Lovers in Blue, Lovers in Grey, Lovers in Pink, Lovers in Green.* 'Don't you miss Paris?' Chagall's friends asked. What could he say?

Sometimes he walked out to visit Grandpa Chagall, who was the rabbi of a country village. Chickens scuttled across the road.

A cow lay in front of Grandpa's house. Someone must have forgotten it was there. How could you forget a cow? Chagall's Paris friends would never believe that an artist could work in these surroundings, among clumsy log houses, bare earth roads, cowpats – and family arguments going on all the time! Chagall was pleased he'd found a quiet studio away from home.

Bella's family owned three jewellery shops. Mrs Rosenfeld wasn't keen on the idea of her beautiful, well-educated daughter marrying the son of a man who worked in the herring factory.

'Marc is a nice boy. But he's got his head in the clouds. Did you ever meet an artist who made a proper good living? *Did* you … Bella! Why is it you don't listen to your mother?'

'After we're married,' Chagall promised Bella, 'we'll fly away to Paris.'

That was in July 1914. In August the First World War broke out. Germany was fighting France to the west and Russia to the east. There was no way the lovers could reach Paris. But they could still get married. The date was set for July 1915.

Bella wanted to give her husband-to-be a special present for his birthday, which was on the sixth of July, three weeks before the wedding. She baked a honey cake and a redcurrant tart. She picked a bouquet of roses and wildflowers, and wrapped the presents in two shawls embroidered with beautiful patterns. She put on her best black dress with the lacy collar. Chagall never forgot the moment that Bella appeared, carrying the presents. 'Blue air, love and flowers floated with her through the window!' he recalled.

Being in love – it was like floating. To anyone else, it would have looked like an ordinary scene. Bella put the food on the table. She was searching for a vase for the flowers. 'Do you like your presents?' she asked. 'Of course I like my presents. They're wonderful. But if you'd given me a pickled herring I'd have been delighted!' Chagall knew he must paint this moment – the bright flowers, the patterned shawls, but most of all the floating feeling. And Bella's gaze when she thought he was standing behind her, then suddenly she was looking into his eyes, as though he had flown from the other side of the room without her knowing. And when Chagall glanced down at the old table and the bare wooden floor, they'd turned red. Red! *Krasnyi!* – which is also very like the Russian word for beautiful.

'Happy birthday!' they both exclaimed at once.

Bicycle Wheel
1951 (copy of the lost original of 1913)

54
Spinning a Story
Marcel Duchamp

Paris was full of bicycles. They bumped over cobblestones, leaned against walls. Yet nobody seemed to realise what a beautiful thing a bicycle wheel is. A perfect circle! A flower of fine, taut metal spokes. Marcel Duchamp found a wheel from a broken bicycle. He took it to his studio. He turned it upside down. He slotted the end of the metal fork holding the wheel through a hole in the seat of a wooden stool. He sat in his armchair and looked at it.

It was perfect. There was nothing he wanted to add. Nothing he wanted to take away. The wheel had been made in a factory, with thousands of others. But when he looked at it like this, in a new light ... 'Well,' he thought, 'if I call this a work of art, who can prove I'm wrong?'

That was in 1913. When war broke out the following year, Duchamp tried to join the French army, but the army doctors said, 'You're no good. You've got a weak heart.' He couldn't just hang around, though, while his friends fought and died. He boarded a steamship bound for New York.

And here he was, sitting on a snow-covered bench in Central Park, reading a letter from his sister, Suzanne. The war in Europe was still raging. The American newspapers said that President Wilson was going to arrange a peace conference. If only! If only the war would end! Duchamp worried about his family. Suzanne was working as a nurse in Paris. His brother Raymond was in the army.

Suzanne wrote that she'd finished clearing out his old studio. Why hadn't she kept the studio for herself? Like her three brothers, Suzanne was an artist. Surely she could have asked their father for help with the studio rent. Duchamp wanted to know what she'd done with his bicycle wheel. Could she have thrown it away? He must reply immediately.

Not so long ago Duchamp was a painter – the kind of modern painter who tries out new ideas like Cubism. He was interested in the way Braque and Picasso combined countless different moments of looking in their pictures. He was fascinated by Eadweard Muybridge's photographs of horses galloping, and men and woman running, dancing, jumping. In 1912 Duchamp painted a picture of a woman walking downstairs, which looked a bit like Muybridge's photographs and a bit like a Cubist painting.

That painting and three others were selected for an exhibition in New York. 'Shocking! Nonsense!' What charming things the American critics said about his paintings! No one was more surprised than Duchamp himself to hear that all four had sold. So when he stepped off the steamship in New York Harbor, Duchamp was already something of a celebrity. People wanted to meet 'the eccentric French artist'.

'I don't care if they think my ideas are odd,' Duchamp shrugged. 'I am most definitely not *their* idea of an artist.' To most people, it seemed, an artist was someone who arranged colours, lines and shapes to make a nice picture. But surely a work of art should do something more than please the eye? Duchamp decided that the really essential thing about being an artist was having interesting ideas that make people see things differently.

Sometimes, at a fashionable party, a guest would come up to Duchamp and say, 'I was bowled over by your paintings!' 'Thank you,' he would reply. 'Perhaps you can help me. I've been wondering, what is it that makes a painting different from a bicycle wheel?' He often got the same answer. 'A painting is unique. It's painted by an artist, and no other painting is exactly the same. A bicycle wheel is produced by machines in a factory. It's identical to all the other wheels.'

'I'm the artist, not you,' thought Duchamp. 'I'm the one who decides what is art.' When you think about it, oil paint comes out of a paint factory in tubes. Artists squeeze paint out of the tubes and spread it around on canvas or paper with a brush and say, 'This is a work of art.' Instead of buying paint in a special shop for artists, Duchamp might decide to buy something else in an ordinary shop. For example, he could go to a hardware shop and buy … 'Let me see …'

Scrape. Scratch. Scrape. A workman was shovelling snow off the path right beside the bench where Duchamp was sitting.

'A snow shovel. Yes! And when I call that shovel art, people will see it as they've never seen it before.'

He pictured Suzanne, sitting in his armchair, gazing at his bicycle wheel, as if she were right there in front of him, even though she was on the far side of the Atlantic. The thought made him feel hopeful. For a moment he forgot about the war.

Designs for Sports Clothing
1923

55
Comrades!
Varvara Stepanova

'Stay still, Aleksandr! Stop laughing or I'm going to stick this pin in your neck!'

Varya balances on a stool, gripping a sheet of red paper in one hand and a pin in the other. She is trying to attach the red paper to a white piece that's pinned around her husband's neck. He stands like a mad magician, staring ahead, both arms outstretched. His face is serious, but his shoulders tremble with laughter. The piece of paper – a sewing pattern that Varya has cut out – falls to the floor.

'It's hopeless!' She's giggling too now. 'Pull yourself together. Imagine … imagine you are listening to a rousing speech by Comrade Lenin.'

Varya – or Varvara Stepanova to give her her full name – is designing clothing for sports. It's a completely new type of sportswear – not white and boring and respectable, like the summer clothes that well-off people wear. No. Varya's designs have strong, colourful patterns that will be like a moving picture when athletes run and jump. Bold red, white and black stripes, a red star. Like flags fluttering in the wind, inspiring the spectators.

Her husband, Aleksandr Rodchenko, is also an artist. He's designing posters, pamphlets, books – all kinds of things that are needed by Russia's revolutionary government. When people ask what he's doing, Rodchenko explains, 'An engineer works with machines.

An architect works with concrete, steel and glass. Artists are working with shapes, colours and lines to construct a new world!'

Varya agrees. 'Today,' she says, 'we artists no longer work all on our own, drawing and painting in our studios. We work alongside designers, architects, engineers, teachers, leaders of the people. We are all striving towards the same goal, helping to construct a modern nation. It's time to stop using the old-fashioned word "artist". We are all Constructivists!'

Stepanova met Rodchenko when they were students at art school in the city of Kazan. At that time they both wanted to be painters. Both of them came from poor families, and it was a great achievement to win a place at Kazan Art School. This was an exciting, turbulent time in Russia. The age-old style of government, with the tsar or emperor at the top, had not adapted to the modern world of factories and cities. 'A revolution is coming,' people whispered. By 1917 they were shouting, 'The Revolution is here!'

Stepanova and Rodchenko were on the side of the Revolution. Its leader, Lenin, proclaimed that Russia was now a new nation where everything would be done differently. Factories and farms would belong to the workers, not the bosses. No one would have to pay to go to school or see a doctor. Before the Revolution, activities like playing sports and going to the theatre had been for just a few people who could afford them. Now they would be for everyone.

Varya remembers arriving in Moscow for the first time, before the Revolution. She remembers the deep, echoing song of the bells ringing from church towers with their golden domes. Today there are no church bells. Instead, in the streets, there are voices booming through megaphones, making speeches. 'Comrades! Comrades!' There is so much hope. But there is fear too. Away from Moscow, in other corners of the old Russian Empire, the Red Army is fighting a civil war against the so-called White Russians, who oppose the Revolution. Soldiers are constructing a new world with guns, killing the enemies of change. Varya glances at the drawings she has made for the sportswear. Red, white – lively, stirring patterns. The artist's way is better …

'Art is a noble calling,' her professor at art school used to say. She could tell that he didn't really expect her or the other girls to become professional artists. He probably expected that they would get married and perhaps do a little bit of painting in their spare time.

How different it is now! The leaders of the Revolution say that everyone is equal. This means that a woman artist is respected as much as a man. All that matters is producing something useful – clothes for workers, fabrics printed with patterns that are sharp and bright as new ideas.

At last she's pinned all the bits of the paper costume together. She will have to make some changes to the white V shape before she gives it to the dressmaker to sew together. Eventually the fabric will be printed in a factory, thousands of tunics will be produced. Rodchenko, meanwhile, is setting up his box camera. This is his latest enthusiasm.

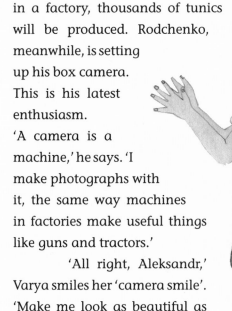

'A camera is a machine,' he says. 'I make photographs with it, the same way machines in factories make useful things like guns and tractors.'

'All right, Aleksandr,' Varya smiles her 'camera smile'. 'Make me look as beautiful as a tractor!'

Moscow

Russia (1930s)

After the Russian Revolution, the old Russian Empire of the tsars became the Soviet Union. Moscow remained the capital city. In keeping with the new spirit in society, architects built new, modern buildings, very different from the old buildings in the historic centre of the city.

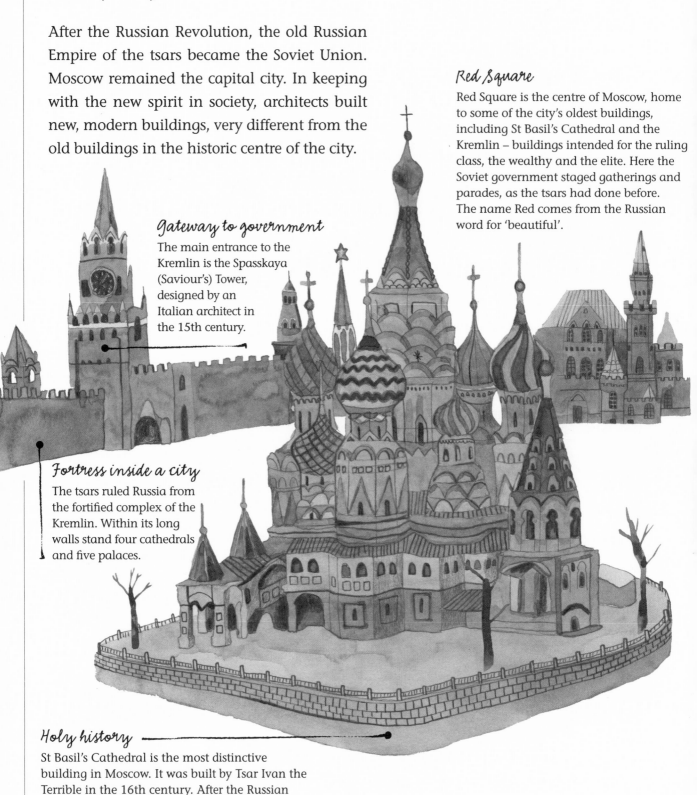

Red Square

Red Square is the centre of Moscow, home to some of the city's oldest buildings, including St Basil's Cathedral and the Kremlin – buildings intended for the ruling class, the wealthy and the elite. Here the Soviet government staged gatherings and parades, as the tsars had done before. The name Red comes from the Russian word for 'beautiful'.

Gateway to government

The main entrance to the Kremlin is the Spasskaya (Saviour's) Tower, designed by an Italian architect in the 15th century.

Fortress inside a city

The tsars ruled Russia from the fortified complex of the Kremlin. Within its long walls stand four cathedrals and five palaces.

Holy history

St Basil's Cathedral is the most distinctive building in Moscow. It was built by Tsar Ivan the Terrible in the 16th century. After the Russian Revolution it became a historical museum.

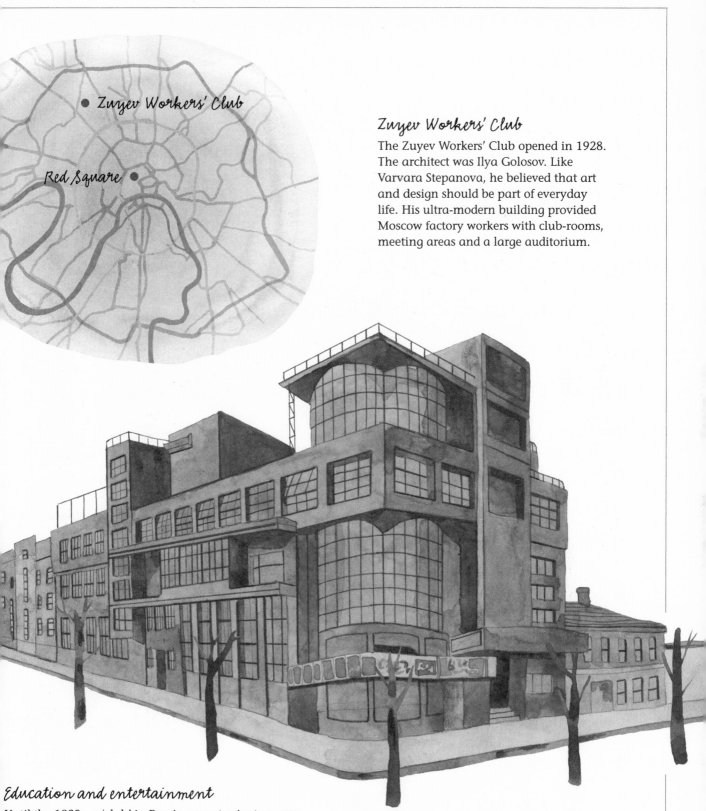

● Zuyev Workers' Club

Red Square ●

Zuyev Workers' Club

The Zuyev Workers' Club opened in 1928. The architect was Ilya Golosov. Like Varvara Stepanova, he believed that art and design should be part of everyday life. His ultra-modern building provided Moscow factory workers with club-rooms, meeting areas and a large auditorium.

Education and entertainment

Until the 1920s, a 'club' in Russia meant private rooms that could be used only by nobles or wealthy people. Workers' clubs like the Zuyev were something new, a place where ordinary people could meet after work to read books, watch films, listen to lectures and hold meetings. They were built in neighbourhoods where working people lived.

New society, new buildings

After the Russian Revolution, artists, architects and designers saw themselves as helping to construct a new society. Architects designed new, modern buildings with glass and concrete, rather than more traditional materials like the bricks used to build St Basil's Cathedral.

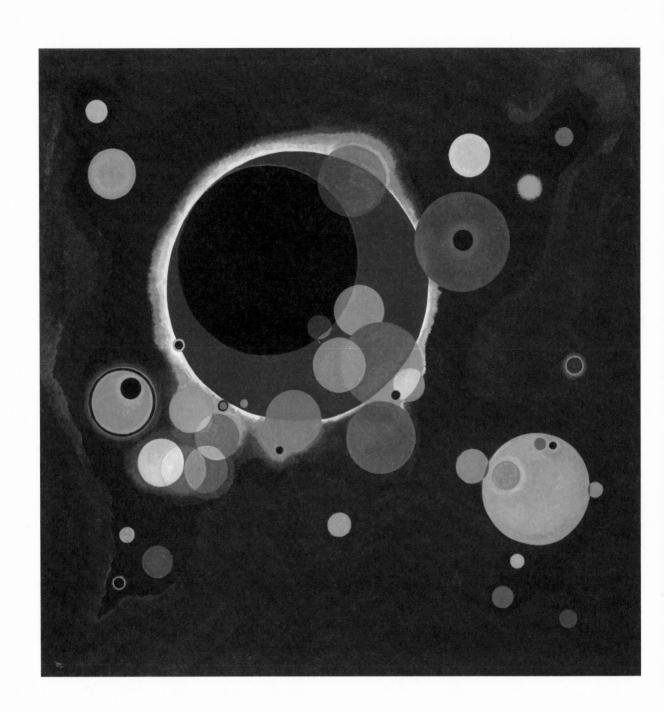

Several Circles
1926

56
Circles of Life
Vasily Kandinsky

The windowpanes were covered with feathery ice, but indoors it looked warm. As soon as Vasily and Nina Kandinsky moved into their new house, they'd painted the walls – a different colour in each room, with a bright red rail up the stairs. The house stood in a grove of pine trees on the edge of the city of Dessau in Germany. Nearby was the Bauhaus, the famous school of design where Kandinsky was a professor of Painting. That too was a brand-new modern building, with flat roofs and vast glass windows.

'Many happy returns!' Nina handed her husband his breakfast cup of coffee and his birthday card.

'Oh please, my dear! Don't remind me.' Kandinsky stared glumly at the circle of steaming black liquid. The years had crept up on him. And now, in December 1926, he was 60 years old. 'If you want to give me a birthday treat, turn the clock back!'

'I'll see what I can do,' Nina smiled. 'Perhaps those young geniuses in the Engineering Science class will be able to help. But when should they turn the clock back *to*?'

Kandinsky fell silent. He pushed his coffee spoon around on the shiny table-top as though drawing an invisible map of his life. Would he really want to start again at the beginning? Growing up in Odessa, studying law in Moscow, finally going to art school in Munich – 30 years ago! It had taken a while for him to find his path as an artist.

He'd spent a lot of time painting in the Bavarian countryside south of Munich. Deep blue mountains, rosy-yellow clouds, red houses. It must have been about 1910 when he realised that, as far as painting was concerned, it was colours and shapes that really mattered to him, echoing the way he felt inside. The colours and shapes didn't need to look like trees, lakes, roads or even human figures.

Colours are like musical sounds, Kandinsky thought. Lemon yellow is a shrill trumpet note. Deep red is a rich cello sound. And certain colours are suited to certain shapes. For deep blue, for example, a rounded shape is best. For a sharp colour like lemon yellow, an angular shape works better than a curved one. In 1912 Kandinsky published a book about his ideas. He saw it all so clearly. Artists could not go on simply copying what was in front of them. They must use the pure materials of art – colours, shapes and lines.

That was an exciting time. Maybe, though, he didn't need to go back so far? Nine years would be enough. That would take him back to Russia, just after the Revolution, when Comrade Kandinsky worked alongside his friends Stepanova and Rodchenko. He became quite an important person, helping to decide about how art was going to build the new world of equality for all. But people whispered behind his back. 'Kandinsky's too wrapped up his own weird ideas to serve the Revolution.' Time to move on again.

Life was better here, in Dessau, he decided. Students listened seriously to his ideas. He taught them how everything a painter needs to do can be done with pure colours, shapes and lines. There's no need to bring faces or flowers, horses or steam trains into your paintings. People sometimes called this sort of painting 'abstract' and said it was hard to understand. If only they would open their eyes! Kandinsky pushed the blue saucer of his coffee cup till its edge almost touched the side of the white envelope with his birthday card from Nina. Across the envelope he placed the silver butter knife with its orange handle …

The Bauhaus was no ordinary art school. It was a place where artists, designers, printers, engineers, dancers and people with all kinds of skills came together to teach and learn. Some of Kandinsky's students would become painters. Others would design furniture, houses, books, coffee pots … His ideas would find their way into art galleries, factories, shops and people's homes.

'Forget what I said, my dear,' he looked up at his wife. 'Today I am as happy as any man deserves to be.'

'Oh good! A smile at last! Let's go out.' Nina helped him on with his overcoat.

In the open space in front of the new Bauhaus building students were having a snowball fight. That was another excellent thing about the Bauhaus. The students were encouraged to have fun – to put on plays, to dance, to party! When they saw Kandinsky approaching, some of them stopped their game.

'Happy birthday, Professor!' they called.

Whump! A snowball hit Kandinsky right on the chest. He looked down. On the glossy black cloth a pure white circle was already melting.

'You just wait!' he shouted. Putting on his 'fierce professor face', he bent down, a little stiffly, and scooped up a fistful of snow.

Self-Portrait on the Border between Mexico and the United States
1932

57

The Girl Between Worlds

Frida Kahlo

It's just a piece of tin, a small oblong sheet. The kind of tin sheet that Mexican painters use for holy pictures called *retablos*.

Frida Kahlo has watched these painters in their little shops. They paint the same figures again and again. They do it so skilfully, so patiently. Jesus spreads out his arms, or his mother, Mary, gazes down at her baby. The *retablo* painters don't earn much, but they must enjoy seeing the blissful expressions on their customers' faces when they've bought a picture. It's as if they could hear Jesus saying, 'Don't worry. As long as you have this *retablo*, I'll be there, looking after you.'

Frida is sitting up in bed with the tin sheet propped in front of her and her paints on the bedside table. It's the only place she can get comfortable. Standing is painful. Sitting is painful. Sometimes the pain fades. This morning it's bad. One day, when she was 18, she jumped on a bus, the same bus she often took. The bus crashed into a tram, and Frida nearly died. The doctors saved her life, but her body never completely healed.

That was when Frida began to paint. She was in bed for months. Painting helped her forget the pain. When she painted her own portrait, it was like putting the pieces of herself back together. And yet, every time she painted a self-portrait, the pieces came together in a different way. 'Who am I?' she wondered. 'I am many Fridas. Which is the true one? They are all true in their way.' Sometimes she likes her own face. Sometimes she hates the sight of it – her big, dark eyes that can never hide her emotions, her thick eyebrows that meet in the middle.

As soon as she woke up this morning, she had an idea for another self-portrait. This time she'll be wearing a pretty dress, like a girl going to a ball. With tiny dabs of paint on the smooth tin sheet Frida paints herself in a pale pink dress.

'You're Cinderella!' her husband Diego exclaims, when he comes to say goodbye and she shows him the painting.

'I wish!' Frida exclaims. 'If only my prince wanted to stay with me instead of running away all the time.'

'You have a good rest.' He stands there with his hat on, gripping his suitcase. 'I'll see you next week.'

Diego Rivera is a big man. He paints enormous murals on the walls of schools, government buildings, factories. In Mexico there are still many people who can't read, but they can learn about their country's history from Rivera's murals. They learn how the Mexican Revolution was a good thing. The old government took advantage of the people. The new government looks after them. That's the message in Rivera's murals.

Rivera has been asked to paint murals in America too. When she's well enough, Frida accompanies him. She knows Mexicans who dream of emigrating to America. They dream of finding work in the factories, of buying a car and having electric lights at home instead of oil lamps. Her Mexican friends tell her 'Our country needs to modernise! We're living in the past. America is the future!'

She looks at her little painting. She thinks, 'In my Cinderella dress I'm going to the ball. The dancers dance to the rhythm of machines. The smoke from the car factory smells of money.'

The girl in the pink dress turns away from the stinking factories. She turns towards the ruined Aztec temple and the broken statue of a skeleton. She turns towards the strange naked gods and the wildflowers and cactuses that sprout up from the soil of Mexico and the sun and the moon with lightning forking between them. But who is she, this Frida – this girl who waves the Mexican flag and holds a cigarette?

To the right of her, the new factories and skyscrapers of America. To the left, the ancient land of Mexico. Frida's painting is like a pair of scales. Which side is heavier? Which will she choose in the end? She mixes orange-red paint with a little yellow and white to make the coral colour for her necklace, the one Rivera bought her in the market.

Ow! If feels like a knitting needle is poking into her back. Frida takes a deep breath. Count to ten. One, two, three …

In the mirror on the other side of the room a young woman sits up in bed. This poorly person stares at Frida as though she could see deep inside her, like an x-ray – her heart, her bones, her secrets. Frida puts down her brush. 'Cheer up, my friend!' she says quietly.

The interesting-looking woman in the mirror smiles back. She understands.

Hirondelle Amour

1933–34

58

Sea of Dreams

Joan Miró

Goodbye, England! Joan Miró leaned over the rail and watched the water churning as the ferry steamed into the English Channel. His thoughts turned to home. Civil war could break out in Spain any day, they said. And in the rest of Europe, what would happen? The speeches of the German leader, Adolf Hitler, were becoming more and more aggressive. The German army had marched right up to the border with France.

Miró looked away from the seething white water. A swallow flew past, its quick wings almost brushing the deck before it sped back towards the land. 'A lucky sign,' he thought without knowing why. What was that bird called in English? *Hirondelle* was the French name. He'd used it in the title of one of his four enormous paintings for Madame Cuttoli, *Hirondelle Amour*. These paintings were designs for tapestries. Madame Cuttoli had a successful fashion business in Paris, and she often asked artists to design things for her.

A word has its own atmosphere, like a colour. *Hirondelle* was a beautiful word, like a little bell ringing. *Amour*, the French word for love, was deep and luminous, like the sea below him. Miró imagined the weird creatures that might be swimming towards the surface or sinking down to their strange homes on the seabed.

He walked up and down the deck. On the whole, his visit to London had gone well. Whether people liked it or loathed it, the exhibition of Surrealist art that opened in June 1936 had definitely caused a stir. But now he couldn't wait to get back to his studio.

Almost a century had passed since Gustave Courbet's paintings caused a stir in Paris. Then came the Impressionists, then Van Gogh and Gauguin, then the Cubists. There seemed no end to the new kinds of art that sprang up in Paris, one after another. Now it was the turn of the Surrealists.

'Do you think of me as a Surrealist?' Miró asked Madame Cuttoli. 'I'm not sure I want to be any kind of "ist".'

'If a Surrealist is a painter of dreams, then yes, you definitely are one.'

'It's not quite so simple,' Miró sighed. The French writer André Breton had invented the word Surrealist. He'd set out what a Surrealist artist should do. At first Miró was excited by Breton's ideas. Now they seemed a bit too much like a set of rules.

Still, he believed it was true – as Breton said – that our deepest wishes and feelings are expressed in dreams. If artists could capture the essence of dreams, they could capture the deepest workings of the human mind. The important thing was not to let your sensible, practical daytime mind blot out the dream pictures.

Miró didn't think that *Hirondelle Amour* was a dream picture exactly. Red, yellow and grey – these colours weren't imaginary, they were real. As real as a matchbox or a newspaper! Miró sometimes took pages from a newspaper and tore them into all sorts of rough shapes. He stuck the shapes onto a piece of cardboard. Real shapes, real cardboard. But a few days later, when he looked at them again, the shapes seemed to turn into birds flying, a man reaching up, a star tumbling out of the sky.

Could he explain where these images came from? No! It's not an artist's job to explain. Nor could Miró explain why ordinary things often seemed to him to have a life of their own. A matchbox or an axe sometimes seemed to him just as alive as a person. That was how he'd felt about objects ever since he was a child. What more could he say?

'Feel your own way forward,' his teacher at art school told him. He thought that Miró had a natural sense of colour but that his line drawings were rather awkward. The teacher made him wear a blindfold and touch the objects he was drawing instead of looking at them. Perhaps that was why he always felt that his pictures were like dreams – bright colours and freely moving lines that he could see perfectly clearly with his eyes shut.

The coast of England was shrinking to a misty grey line on the northern horizon. Miró searched the southern horizon for the shape of France. He was impatient to get back to Paris, where he had lived for the past few years. Much further south, at his family's farm in Tarragona, the swallows would be feeding their young in nests under the eaves.

When the swallows returned next year, would they see the same peaceful fields below them? Or would they see burning buildings and holes made in the fields by bombs?

Thick smoke trailed from the ship's funnel like sooty writing, dissolving in the distance before it could tell him the answer.

Guernica
1937

59
The Lie that Tells the Truth

Pablo Picasso

It was April 1937. I was having breakfast with Pablo Picasso at a pavement café. A man at the next table leaned across, waving a copy of the *Times*.

'Have you seen the terrible news from Spain?' he asked in English, pointing to an article in the paper.

'What's he saying?' Picasso doesn't speak English, but he heard the word 'Spain'. Every day there was news of the civil war that had broken out the year before in Picasso's native country, when the army led by General Franco turned against the government. Picasso was safe in Paris, but he still had many friends in Spain. The city of Barcelona, where he'd been an art student, had seen fierce fighting.

I took the newspaper and did my best to translate the article. It described an air raid two days before on the town of Guernica in northern Spain. The reporter had seen the effects of the bombing with his own eyes. 'Guernica was completely destroyed by air raiders,' I translated slowly. 'The bombing lasted three hours. Fighter planes flew low, shooting people who were trying to escape. Many of the casualties are women and children.' Helped by Hitler's airforce, General Franco was trying out a new kind of warfare, the reporter said.

On the way back to the studio, Picasso was silent. I could tell he was thinking about Guernica, imagining the explosions, the panic everywhere. He felt burning anger, but what could he do to help?

Already at that time, Picasso was the most famous living artist in the world. There was huge demand for his work. The Spanish government had asked him to paint a mural for the Spanish Pavilion at the World's Fair, which was soon to take place in Paris. They hoped that, by involving Picasso and other well-known artists, they would make people aware of the terrible suffering caused by the war in Spain.

After hearing the news about Guernica, Picasso knew what he would paint. He would paint a picture that was so shocking, so mesmerising that no one would be able to turn away. They wouldn't be able to say any more, 'We don't really know what's going on in Spain. It's none of our business, is it?' People would be so appalled by the story of Guernica that, somehow, the violence would be stopped.

Picasso stretched an enormous canvas right across his studio, from side to side and floor to ceiling. It was more than 3 metres tall and 7 metres wide. It seemed impossible that a single artist could finish a picture this size in time for the World's Fair, which was only a month away.

In the streets and parks outside, Paris was at its most lovely as spring turned to summer. Inside the studio it was another world. Picasso worked like a man possessed. Before he began the vast painting, he made many drawings, trying out different arrangements of figures. Then he got to work, drawing the outlines on the canvas, then starting to paint. He didn't use any bright colours – only black and white and grey. Up and down a ladder he went. In the middle of the canvas he painted the head of a screaming horse. On the left he drew a bull, and a woman clasping a dead child. A wounded man lay on the ground. Shouting heads swooped from the shadows like ghosts.

Sometimes Picasso asked me, 'Dora, can you help with this bit? In the corner, there.' But most of the time I watched. I got my camera and photographed Picasso as he worked. He was constantly changing things as he went along. He changed a blazing sun into a lightbulb, and lifted up the head of the screaming horse from near the bottom of the painting to the top. Even when Picasso had his back turned, I felt the intensity of his concentration. Painting that huge mural would have kept ten artists busy, but here was Picasso, all alone and completely in charge.

And yet what was he doing? When the painting was finished, it didn't look anything like a war photograph, with bombed buildings and bodies in the streets. The shrieking, broken figures and jagged shapes twisted my heart. 'Why is that bull there?' I asked Picasso. 'Whose is that arm, holding a lamp?'

Picasso would never give a straight answer to questions like these. 'You should know by now, Dora,' he said. 'Art is the lie that tells the truth.'

When I saw *Guernica* in the Spanish Pavilion at the World's Fair, its impact was even more powerful than it had been in the studio. I thought how easy it is for a pilot to open the hatch in a plane so that bombs tumble down onto helpless people far below. But who could make a painting like that, a great dark explosion of anger and pity? Only Picasso!

Platform scene of sleeping people.
3 or 4 people under one blanket — uncomfortable positions, distorted
Foreshortenings — All kinds & colours of blankets, sheets & old coats
Two figures in sleeping embrace
Masses of sleeping figures fading to perspective point of the tunnel.
Groups of people sleeping, disorganised angles of arms & legs. covered
here & there with blankets.

Three Figures Sleeping:
Study for 'Shelter Drawing'
1940–41

60

Pebbles and Bombs

Henry Moore

The pebble comes from a beach in Norfolk. It is perfectly smooth, like a giant egg, but flatter and heavier. He likes to hold it in both hands with his eyes shut. Feel the shape. Feel the weight. How many years did it take the sea to smooth this lump of stone – thousands? Millions? In his head he hears the clunky rattle of pebbles tumbling against each other on the beach as the waves churn over them and slip back again.

Those were great holidays, Henry Moore remembers. He'd go to the Norfolk seaside with his friends – most of them were artists too. Back in his studio, he would carve a sculpture until it was smooth as a pebble. A head, elbows, shoulders, knees. A sculpture should look as though it has been shaped by the sea, the wind, by time itself – not by fiddly little chips and scrapes of a chisel. The human body is made of hills and valleys. He imagines the land as a sleeping person, as though the horizon were rising and falling ever so slightly with each breath.

Moore's father worked in a coal mine. There were eight children, and they all lived in a tiny house near the mine. Two beds, with four children in each bed. 'Study hard, and you can have a better life,' their father was always telling them. Homework. Violin lessons. Art school. Moore became a sculptor.

'I don't understand why a lad with your education has to sweat away with a hammer and chisel,' his mother said. Was his life

today better than his parents' life? It was different, anyhow.

When he was an art student in London, Moore often visited the British Museum to look at the ancient sculptures. There was a Mexican statue of a man – a warrior or a priest – lying down. His knees were bent, his head lifted, alert and still. 'That's the kind of sculpture I want to carve,' Moore thought, 'not statues of generals and prime ministers.' He filled his sketchbook with drawings of ancient sculptures from Greece, Italy, Mexico and Africa.

Moore got used to hearing people criticise his sculptures. 'My child could do better!' they'd say. Or 'That's the sort of thing a cave man would carve!' He took this as a compliment. He had visited the painted caves that had been discovered at Altamira in Spain and admired the beautiful, powerful figures of bison lit up by the guide's torch.

And there were worse things to worry about than being criticised. In 1939 war broke out again all across Europe. Hitler's armies invaded Poland, then Belgium and France. In September 1940 Hitler's airforce started bombing London, night after night. It was like Guernica, but on a much bigger scale. There weren't enough air raid shelters, so Londoners went down every evening into the Underground, seeking safety on station platforms and in the deep train tunnels.

Moore puts the pebble back on the windowsill. He checks his bag to make sure that he's packed his sketchbook, pencils and paint box. Tonight he'll be there too, in the Underground, where people are trying to sleep and the bombs rumble and growl high above in the burning streets. The government has asked artists like Moore to record how people are carrying on their lives in the midst of so much fear and destruction.

Every night it's the same. Children, parents, grandparents – everybody gathers in the Underground. They find a space on the platform, or in the bunk beds that the government has started to set up. Toys, books, blankets, food, drink – they do their best to make themselves cosy. Often there's music. Someone sings or plays the accordion or a banjo, but at last it quietens down. There'll be babies crying, people snoring, coughing, farting. The stuffy, smelly, blanket-covered land of sleep. Forget about the bombs. Forget about what you'll find when you come out into the street tomorrow.

Moore tries not to stare too long and hard. He doesn't want to attract attention as he draws in his sketchbook, quickly, quietly, sometimes writing notes beside a picture. Later, in his studio, he'll turn these rapid little sketches into finished drawings, with all the lines and shading. Thousands of years ago, he thinks, cave people looked just the same asleep as we look now. There are sleepers with arms flung across their faces or clasped behind their heads, curled up on their sides, hugging their children – in all kinds of positions.

A trickle of dust falls from the platform's curved ceiling. Surely they are safe down here? Staring into the mouth of a disused tunnel, Moore can make out shadowy figures and the glow-worm lights of cigarettes. It's as though he can see his father with his friends, going down the mine. Suddenly, in this strange place, he feels at home.

Merzbau
Hanover, Germany, about 1923–33 (destroyed 1943)

61
It's All Rubbish!
Kurt Schwitters

Attention! The electrical pyjamas will sneeze tomorrow. Dogs must telephone in eight colours.

Kurt Schwitters woke with a start. He'd been laughing in his sleep. Again. He kept dreaming about those crazy poems. It was 25 years ago, yet the words popped into his dreams as though he were pulling them from a hat right there and then.

Yes, pulling them from a hat. It was Tristan Tzara's idea – his Romanian friend and fellow inventor of bizarre forms of art. You cut an article from a newspaper. You snip it up into single words, put the words in a hat, shake it around a bit. Then you take the words out one by one.

'It will make a poem every time!' Tzara insisted. Well, perhaps not every time. But the good poems were brilliant. Schwitters had forgotten almost all the poems his teachers made him learn at school, but he remembered the electrical pyjamas, even in his sleep. If you stick scraps and fragments together, any old how, without thinking about what you're doing, you can get amazing results.

Schwitters rubbed a hole in the mist on the window. Another damp morning in the Lake District. Somewhere out there were the mountains. He could hear sheep baaing in the foggy rain. The smell of burnt toast wafted up from the kitchen. When he'd arrived in Britain in 1940, he was sent straight to a camp for foreigners. He was German, after all, and Britain was at war with Germany. It was useless explaining

that the German leader Hitler wanted to stamp out
artists like Schwitters, who made unusual and
thought-provoking art. In the camp he'd worked
with any materials he could lay his hands on.
He had even made sculptures out of porridge
and toast ...

Scraps and fragments. That was how it had been
in Germany in the years after the First World War ended in 1918.
Soldiers like Schwitters returned home and picked up the pieces as
best they could. Before the war Schwitters had been an art student in
Dresden. Afterwards, he couldn't find anything that an artist would
want to paint. Flowers in a vase? A bowl of fruit? No – all he could see
in the streets were wounded soldiers and hungry, ragged people. It felt
as though the Germany he remembered from his childhood had been
smashed up and all that was left was a rubbish heap.

Schwitters began to make collages out of bits and pieces of
paper – price tags, food labels, whatever caught his eye.
And why stop at paper? Here was a sliver of
painted wood. He could nail that to the
picture. Here was the wooden wheel of a
child's toy, a piece of netting.

If anyone asked Schwitters what
on earth he was doing, he'd reply, 'I'm a
painter. The only difference is, I nail my
pictures together.'

'But artists don't nail their pictures
together!'

'Ah, that's because I am the only
artist who makes *Merz*.'

Merz? What did that mean?
Schwitters had invented the word.
Only he could answer the question.

'This is *Merz*.' He picked a
torn tram ticket off the pavement.

'This is *Merz* too. And this. And this.' A broken wooden crate outside a shop. A bent spoon.

Schwitters went back to live in his parents' house in Hanover. There was plenty of room. And there was no end to the *Merz* that Schwitters kept bringing back home. A chair with two legs. An old shoe. An empty beer bottle. It seemed a shame that there was no piece of paper or canvas or wood big or strong enough to stick all this *Merz* to.

What could he do? He would use the rooms – floors, walls, ceilings, staircases. Inside his parents' house, Schwitters constructed another house made of *Merz*. He called it the *Merzbau*, or 'Merz Building'. Out of pieces of wood and cardboard he constructed caves and arches, secret ledges and spiky roofs. He hid treasures in them – a sweet tin with a picture of a cat, a lock of a friend's hair. The *Merzbau* grew and grew. It would be the size of a cathedral now if he hadn't had to run for it, before Hitler's thugs came looking for him. Schwitters was in England when news reached him that it had all been destroyed – the *Merzbau*, house, and all the streets around, when British and American planes bombed Hanover in 1943.

Now the war was over, it was time to begin again. Later today he would walk along the farm track, through the mist to the barn. Inside the barn, Schwitters had been sticking bits of *Merz* to the end wall. He covered them with plaster to make strange shapes.

But first he must get dressed, have a cup of coffee and scrape the burnt bits off the toast.

Where It's At
1950–2014

Throughout most of history, few people travelled long distances or knew very much about life in other parts of the world. After the Second World War, this changed. Air travel and television, telephones and films, and then the internet, connected people across great distances. Sharing ideas, skills and experiences became much easier.

Art continued to thrive on the skills and experience that come from long traditions, but it also embraced and combined ideas from different times and places. American artist Jackson Pollock was inspired by the strange imagery of the European Surrealists. Australian Aboriginal artist Emily Kame Kngwarreye practised age-old techniques with new materials, using modern acrylic paints to create patterns her people had been using for thousands of years. Ghanaian artist El Anatsui joined together objects and ideas from different parts of the world, producing artworks that look like African royal robes from European and American bottle caps. If artists had ideas that were too big or difficult for one person to make, they got other people involved, like Ai Weiwei and his hundred million sunflower seeds.

Today, new ways of combining materials and techniques, mixing old ideas with new ones, help artists to express their feelings about the world we live in and explore what it means to be human.

Full Fathom Five
1947

62
Straight from the Can
Jackson Pollock

I press my face against the barn wall. The planks smell of tar and sunlight. Through a gap I peek inside. At first I can't see clearly. It's so bright out here. All I can see through my spyhole is Jackson's back and the dusty smoke-curl from his cigarette sliced by a sunbeam.

There are paintings leaning against the walls, but the one he's working on this afternoon lies on the floor. He told me this is how he's going to paint from now on. He'll pin the canvas to the floor so he can walk all round it, so he can get at it from any direction.

Why not? We all have this idea of the artist, brush in hand, sitting or standing face-to-face with their painting. It doesn't have to be that way. Jackson likes how the Navajo sand-painters work, trickling coloured sand onto the bare earth floor to make their sacred patterns.

My eyes adjust. Jackson is sprinkling tin tacks from a little box into his palm. He scatters them over the painting like seeds. He sits down on a crate and stares at the painting. I stand on tiptoe but I can't see what he's staring at. Then he jumps up, grabs an open paint tin from the table, and it all starts again.

We moved out to Long Island from New York City over a year ago, in the fall of 1945, shortly after we got married. Jackson wanted to live near the ocean. He needed wide open spaces, he said. There was a barn on our land that blocked his view of the water. He took it apart and rebuilt it next to the house. Now it's his studio. We don't have electricity, so he can only paint in daylight.

When I first met Jackson he was totally unknown as an artist. I introduced him to other artists. I found him work on government projects. His paintings became bigger and bolder, all swirling lines and spatters of paint, writhing with energy. He started to get noticed. After his first exhibition people said 'Jackson Pollock could be the greatest American painter of our time.' And you have to agree that it *is* high time we had some great American painters. It's time for Europe to admit that America is the future.

Why don't I knock at the door and step inside? I don't want Jackson to know I'm here. I want to see how he paints when he's in his own world, with no thought of anyone watching. He tips up the pot of house paint, and the paint slurps straight out onto the canvas. He dips a wooden stick into another pot, and flicks and drips the paint – here, there, too quick for thinking. All the time, he strides and kind of dances around the canvas, bent over it, a magician casting a spell.

If I knock on the door I'll break the spell. No artist has painted this way before. Not ever. I move a little to the left and get a glimpse of the painting on the floor. The swirls and blobs of thick paint gleam – glossy black, silver, white. What is it all about? You might as well ask a dancer, 'What are you dancing about?' When something takes your breath away, the what's-it-about bit isn't so important.

It's too hot out here. I walk down towards the creek. A breeze comes off the water. Sooner or later I'll get started on a new painting of my own. I'm Lee Krasner, artist, I tell myself, not just plain Mrs Jackson Pollock. The water laps against the shore, making the pebbles shine like jewels.

When I get back, Jackson is prowling outside the studio. He has that creased-up frown of his, like he's expecting to be arrested for murder.

'Tell me what you think,' he demands. 'I don't know what I'm doing.'

I go inside and get my first proper look at his new painting.

'I'm mesmerised,' I say. Jackson stands by my side, like he's trying to see the painting through my eyes. The painting looks as if it's alive, moving, like the paint is going on pouring and spattering itself all on its own. 'Is it finished?' I ask.

'Finished?' he stares at me. 'How would I know?' Suddenly he demands, 'What do you have in your pockets?'

'Uh – not much.' I pull out a couple of coins and a key. Jackson takes them and chucks them into the shining paint trails. He dips a screwdriver into the tin of aluminium paint and waves it over the painting like a pendulum. He walks over to the other side, picks up another tin, lets a long, thin tongue of black paint come trailing out.

'Great!' I say. 'Terrific!'

He sways as he moves, a man in a trance. If he heard what I said, he gives no sign.

New York
United States (1950s)

After the Second World War, New York City overtook Paris as the world capital of modern art. American abstract painters like Jackson Pollock were in great demand. Europe had been shattered by the war, but the American economy was thriving. Wealthy collectors wanted to buy young artists' work as well as historic art.

Getting started

The Art Students League was founded in 1875 as a place where students could learn from professional artists. Louise Bourgeois, Lee Krasner and Jackson Pollock all studied there.

Mother's downstairs

Louise Bourgeois moved from Paris to New York in 1938. She and her family lived in a house on West 20th Street, where she used the basement as her studio.

Louise Bourgeois's house

Waterfront

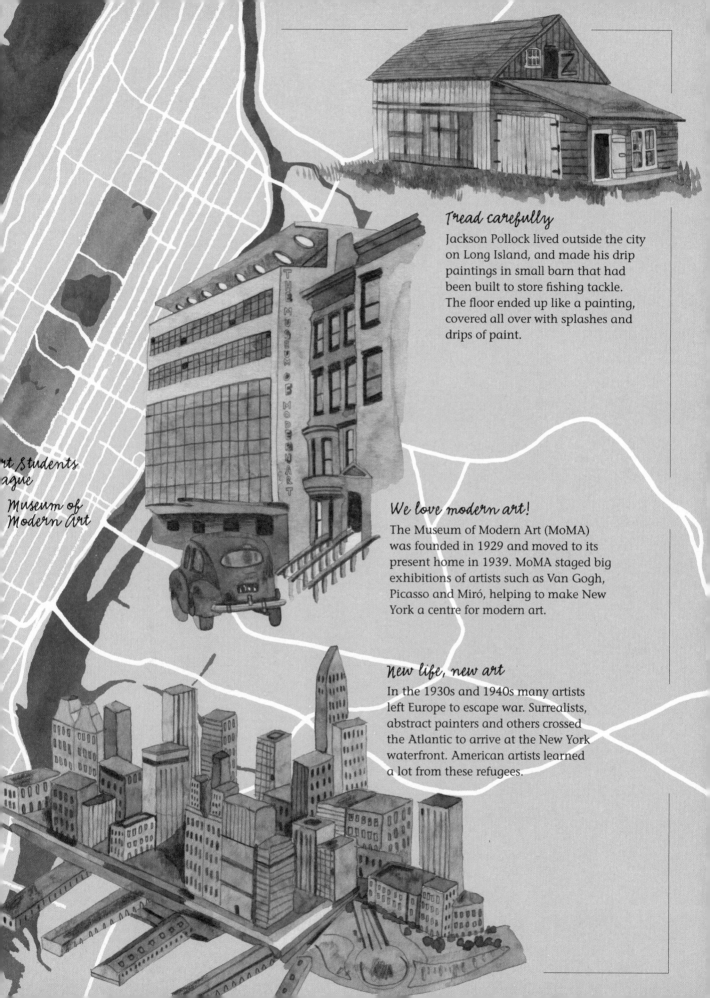

Tread carefully

Jackson Pollock lived outside the city on Long Island, and made his drip paintings in small barn that had been built to store fishing tackle. The floor ended up like a painting, covered all over with splashes and drips of paint.

We love modern art!

The Museum of Modern Art (MoMA) was founded in 1929 and moved to its present home in 1939. MoMA staged big exhibitions of artists such as Van Gogh, Picasso and Miró, helping to make New York a centre for modern art.

New life, new art

In the 1930s and 1940s many artists left Europe to escape war. Surrealists, abstract painters and others crossed the Atlantic to arrive at the New York waterfront. American artists learned a lot from these refugees.

rt Students
ague

Museum of
Modern Art

Tree of Life
1948–51

63
In the Blue Morning
Henri Matisse

What time is it? Henri Matisse must have fallen asleep at last. Across the room, facing his bed, two pale ladders of lilac-grey light show that day is dawning behind the closed shutters. A motorbike putters up the long, steep hill from Nice. Then it's quiet again.

The light gets stronger. The air is warmer already. Matisse watches the lilac-grey turn to glowing yellow-white. Light spreads across the ceiling, like the tide sweeping in across the sand. He wants to spring out of bed and throw open the shutters. Spring? Maybe not. He remembers that he is old. Too many new days have come and gone …

Today he has to take decisions about the new chapel he is designing. It stands on the edge of the town of Vence, in the hills not far away. Paul Bony, who is making the stained glass for the chapel windows, has sent Matisse a box full of small pieces of coloured glass. Every shade of yellow and blue and green. Matisse must choose the exact colours so that the windows can be made. But which yellow? Which blue? Which green?

When it comes to colour, Matisse is king. Long ago, before the First World War, Matisse was one of the young French painters known as *Fauves*, or 'wild beasts' – not because of the way they behaved but because of their outlandish choice of colours. A woman with deep blue hair. A man with a bright green nose. Whatever next?

People imagined that pictures like these were painted by deranged artists with staring eyes and straggly beards. When Matisse turned up in his well-cut suit, neat tie and shiny shoes, they had to think again. Other young artists were also painting in astonishing new ways, like Pablo Picasso and Georges Braque. Now, in 1950, they are old too. Their names appear in history books, which explain about Cubism and the Russian Revolution and the Surrealists and the Second World War.

Gently does it! Slowly, painfully, Matisse sits up in bed. His back hurts. His head aches. He knows what some people say when they compare him to Picasso. 'Matisse paints beautiful pictures, but we do not live in a beautiful world. Think of all the war and suffering that has happened in our lifetimes. Think of Picasso's *Guernica* – that's more like the truth!'

He remembers his visit to Morocco almost 40 years ago. He loved the hot blue sky, the green explosions of palm trees, and the funny way that people relaxed by watching goldfish swimming round in a bowl. Sometimes they'd sit and watch for hours. Was it the bright vermilion colour of the goldfish they liked, or their quiet, flowing movements? Why shouldn't looking at a painting be like that? A painting should make you feel relaxed and refreshed. If you want a basinful of war and suffering, open a newspaper instead.

Around him the bedroom is coming out of the shadows. He can see the vase of flowers on the table, and the glass jug from Venice, and the Chinese bowl. These objects are old friends. He has painted them many times. 'An object is like an actor,' he thinks. 'The same actor can act a different part in many plays.'

He has so much to do! He has made gigantic drawings of the figures that will decorate the chapel walls. He's designing all the stained-glass windows, and the clothes the priests will wear. When everything is finished, the chapel will be a place where your thoughts can be peaceful and free, touched by the coloured light flowing through the windows.

Matisse has designed a window with yellow, leafy shapes that seem to wave gently like seaweed. He has his own way of making these shapes. He paints a big piece of paper yellow. Then he takes an enormous pair of scissors and, turning the paper in his hands, cuts out the shape. 'Drawing with scissors,' he calls it. It is like carving a sculpture out of pure colour. Paul Bony will turn these shapes into stained glass to make the big windows.

He lifts a square of blue glass from the bedside table and squints through it. He does the same with a yellow one. A blue bedroom. A yellow bedroom. They look like two completely different rooms. The yellow is too lemony, though. He tries another yellow, but it is too orangey. Maybe this one? Ah! Just right.

And the blue? Matisse holds a square of deep blue glass up to the light. A beautiful blue! He could look at it for hours and never get tired of it. He has forgotten his aching back and his sore head. He feels young again. A smudge of blue light dances on the tip of his nose.

Landscape with Wing
1981

64
What Happened Here?
Anselm Kiefer

What has happened in this bare, blackened countryside? Has the soil been churned by ploughs and broken up by winter frost? Or has there been a battle, leaving shell holes, tank tracks, clothing and blood and bones mixed into the earth? Anselm Kiefer works brittle straw into the flecked, lumpy surface of his big painting until the earth is as earthy as can be. But still there's the question – what happened here?

Kiefer was born in Germany in March 1945. This should have been a good time to be born. A few weeks later the Second World War ended, and Europe was finally at peace again. But when he thinks back to childhood, he sees ruins everywhere. German cities have been bombed until all that is left are mounds of bricks and stones and burned timbers.

Later he wanted to find out what really happened during the war, before he was born. He learned that people in other countries thought everyone in Germany should be ashamed because of the cruel actions of their leaders. What about his own parents and their friends? Did *they* have any idea what became of their Jewish neighbours after they were rounded up by soldiers? Did they know about the camps where millions of people were killed?

No one seemed to want to answer these questions. 'It's in the past now,' they said. 'It's history. We have to forget about it and move on.'

Kiefer realised that, when you look back at history, you can make up your mind about who is good and who is bad. When you are caught up in events, it's not so clear-cut. What would he have done in their place?

As he couldn't travel back in time, the only way to find out was in his own imagination. Of course there were history books – but history books made too much sense of senseless and terrible events. Myths, on the other hand, told very different kinds of stories. In a myth, a hero can be creative and destructive, good and bad at the same time. Kiefer painted enormous pictures of his studio in the attic with its bare wooden floor and walls. In each picture the studio was empty, except for a spear stuck in the floor, or two swords lying there, as though legendary heroes had just been fighting.

The empty room in his paintings looked like a peaceful place where, only a moment ago, something very violent had happened. It was as if it were waiting for the spirits of dead heroes to return. And perhaps it was. From his childhood after the war, Kiefer remembered the shattered houses where people had once lived, the holes in the ground where houses had stood. But in those days people also worked hard to pick up the pieces and begin again. Even if all you had was a pile of broken bricks, you'd start building.

Kiefer didn't remember being given toys when he was a child, but he did remember playing in ruined buildings, using the bricks to build houses. 'Ruins were not the end,' he thinks. 'They were the beginning of something new.' Maybe that's why he likes to build up his paintings with straw, tar, grit, soil, twigs. Maybe. He stands back to look at the big, earthy painting. Perhaps this is the earth before anything has happened on it,

good or bad. An
artist can dive down into
history, down, down, down to the
very beginning of the world.

Kiefer is making a wing out of
lead. The lead sheet is soft to cut. Each
strip is a flat, grey feather. He spreads
the long metal feathers out, like a bird's
wing in flight. But the beautiful wing is
heavy as a lump of concrete. It will take
some fixing to the painting.

Kiefer has been thinking about Wayland, the master
blacksmith in a Norse myth. Wayland forged metal wings for himself
so that he could escape from imprisonment by the cruel King Nithud.
Wayland is the hero – but before he flies away, he murders Nithud's
three sons, cuts their skulls in half and turns them into drinking cups.
He makes glittering jewellery from their eyes and teeth.

He will fix the wing here, just above the middle of the earthy
landscape. A wing is the opposite of earth. It makes you think of flying,
of being free, as light as air. But a wing made of heavy lead … Surely
Wayland's metal wings would have dragged him down. Or is this
another kind of wing? We talk about our thoughts having wings, flying
wherever they want to, into the future or back to the past. And time,
too – time has wings. But if this is one of the wings of time, why is it
lying in a field? Has time stopped flying? Where have we landed, in this
blackened, earthy place between then and now?

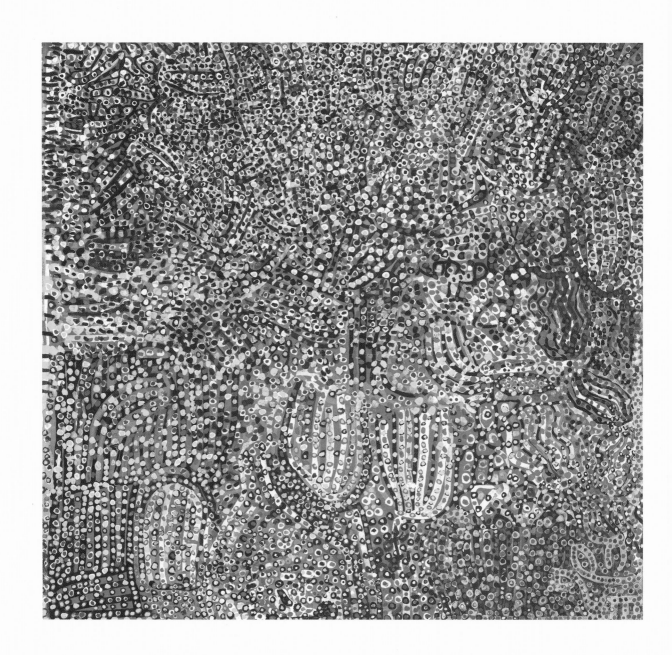

Ntange Dreaming
1989

65

My Dreaming

Emily Kame Kngwarreye

How much can an artist put into a painting? 'The whole lot,' says Emily Kame Kngwarreye. 'The whole lot.'

It's 1989 and she is 78 years old. Or 81. She isn't sure. And does it matter? The whole lot can't be measured in years. Time, all of time from the very beginning, will not fit round it. The place where the Dreamtime spirits came from, before the beginning, and the place where they are now – you won't find such places in your geography books. Put away your map, with its little red and yellow lines for roads and its dull grey spots for towns.

Your map brought you here, through the hot red Western Desert in the middle of Australia. You drove north from Alice Springs to an area called Utopia to meet Emily Kame Kngwarreye. She lives in a small settlement, among her relatives, her clan. Other clans of the Anmatyerre people live in their own settlements not so far away. This is their country. For a while, the white farmers with their cattle tried to take it over. But it's a harsh, dry land where the rain sometimes doesn't fall for years on end. The farmers and most of the cattle have gone.

The Anmatyerre know how to survive here. They know where the food plants grow and how to find yam roots underground. When the rains come, the *ntange* plants flower. If you gather the tiny seeds, you can grind them between stones. The juice is good to drink. The pulp can be shaped into little cakes, to celebrate the coming of the rains.

The Dreamtime spirits shaped this land. They made the *uturupa*, the big sand hill that gave Utopia its name, and created the plants and the soil where the plants grow.

Emily dips her fingers in paint and leans forwards. With her fingertips she makes little spots on the piece of canvas spread in front of her. As she works, the spots multiply, like stars coming out in the night sky or pollen blowing from a flower. These coloured spots are flowers and seeds of the *ntange*. They cover up a pattern of branching lines that Emily has already painted, like the lines painted on dancers' bodies for the rain ceremony. It all happens quickly. She paints as though she is telling a story with her fingers or tracing lines and spots on a mysterious map. Under the shade of these scrubby trees, the wet paint dries quickly in the desert heat.

People often drive out to Utopia from Alice Springs, hoping to buy paintings from Emily. In art galleries in the cities, her paintings fetch high prices. When Emily goes to see them, hanging under the spotlights, they look far away from home, from the place where she paints them, with bright colours against the red desert soil in the blue shade of the trees.

She has become famous. Her paintings have won awards. She shares out the money she earns among the clan. After all, the stories and patterns that Emily paints are their stories and patterns too. The land where the *ntange* grows, and the seeds that are good to eat – these are shared by everyone.

Emily Kame Kngwarreye didn't start to paint until she was over 70. Before that, like many women of her clan, she made batik cloth. She helped to set up the Women's Batik Group. But batik is hard work, especially when you get old. You draw patterns on silk with wax. Then you dye the silk. The colours soak into the unwaxed parts. You boil the silk so the wax melts. You have to get every tiny bit of wax out of the cloth. Hard work! Paintings don't need all that boiling and cleaning. You can concentrate on the patterns and colours. And soon after you put it on the canvas, the acrylic paint is dry.

Perhaps it's a good thing that people in the cities enjoy looking at Emily's paintings on the white walls of art galleries. If they like her paintings, does it really matter why they enjoy them? They will never scrape and dig in the red soil to find yam roots, or gather *ntange* seeds, or paint patterns on their bodies and dance for the spirits who make the *ntange* flowers bloom.

Ntange Dreaming, Emily decides to call her painting. It's a way of thanking the Dreamtime spirits who shaped the land and who look after it, always. Or it's a beautiful pattern hanging on a white wall. It depends who you are, she thinks, and where you are standing.

If you could stay here, in Utopia, you'd find Emily in the same place tomorrow, beginning a new painting. But it's time to leave. Night falls quickly in the desert. The temperature suddenly drops. In the clear, deep sky the stars come out, first one, then three or four, then the whole lot.

Cell (Choisy)
1993

66
Come Inside
Louise Bourgeois

A golden childhood. That's what people think when they see the family photographs. Look at that big house. Imagine the elegant rooms, where summer breezes blow through from the garden that runs down to the River Seine. Look at the girls with their long hair and white dresses. Girls who can no doubt have whatever they want. A pony? Of course! A new party frock? Why not! The elegant house is in France, in a place called Choisy-le-Roi. So romantic!

Ah! That's how it looks from outside. For Louise Bourgeois, it was a nightmare. A nightmare of worry and shame and anger that she can never forget.

It is 1993 and Louise Bourgeois's childhood was long, long ago. She hid underneath the dining-room table, watching her parents' legs walk this way and that, hearing their voices – her father's angry, her mother's sad. She remembers going with her mother to visit her

father, who was wounded in the First World War. She remembers the sounds of an army hospital at night. Black. Black. In these memories everything is coloured black.

Her father came home. But he did not come home a nice man. He came back messed up by fighting and being wounded and losing so many friends. 'What are you?' she saw him thinking. 'You're just a girl. A girl is nothing!'

Louise grew up. She studied mathematics at university in Paris. She travelled to Russia. She met an American called Robert. They married and went to live in New York. That was 1938. Even that was a long time ago. Louise missed her sister and friends in France. She felt emptiness around her. She filled the emptiness with figures made from wood. These were the first sculptures that she showed in an art gallery.

'An Exhibition by Louise Bourgeois'. That sounded good. But still she guessed what people were thinking: 'Not bad. Not bad, considering she's only a woman.' She looked around her at the other artists in New York, the artists who were being talked about, like Jackson Pollock. They were all men. It made her angry. Even more, it made her determined.

She sometimes got so worked up she could have burst into flames. Yet her body stood there, breathing, gurgling, going on with its life the same as usual, while her feelings ran riot. She made sculptures that looked like bits of bodies – fingers, breasts, mysterious wobbly wodges of fat and flesh. Before this, most sculptures of human beings showed what we look like from the outside. Louise Bourgeois' sculptures, on the other hand – they were like being inside your own body. Or being a tiny baby looking at its mother's enormous body, a body as big as the world.

Maybe everything we feel when we grow up goes back to our earliest feelings about the world we've been born into – its unfamiliar shapes, sounds and smells. Louise remembered very clearly how she felt when she was little. Home is a weird place. Grown-ups are weird creatures, who can make the sun shine or the storm clouds rumble.

At the age of 81, Louise Bourgeois is famous for her sculptures. All over the world museums and galleries want to have exhibitions by

Louise Bourgeois. But when she leaves her home in the morning and walks through the New York streets to her studio, nobody stops and stares. They push on in a hurry, past the old lady with her long face, sharp little eyes and woolly beret. 'My ideas, they are big!' she laughs. 'But if you see me, I am like a mouse behind a radiator!'

Luckily her studio is big enough for her ideas. Here are her 'Cells'. They are like rooms into which you cannot go. You can only walk around them and peep in from outside. Why has she called them 'Cells'? Cells are what our bodies are made of. They are where holy people think and pray, or where prisoners are locked up, cut off from everyone else.

Who is imprisoned in this Cell, with its wire fence all round? It's not a person but a dolls' house. A dolls' house of pink marble that you can't touch or step inside. It is the house in the family photographs, where Louise grew up. Above the wire fence hangs the huge blade of a guillotine, like the one that cut off the head of the King of France in the French Revolution.

'It shows how the present is cut off from the past,' Louise explains.

She looks at the house where she grew up. It is small in the distance, like a house in a dream. Under its stone roof, behind its stone windows, she hears her parents' voices, her father's angry and her mother's sad, as she crouches under the table.

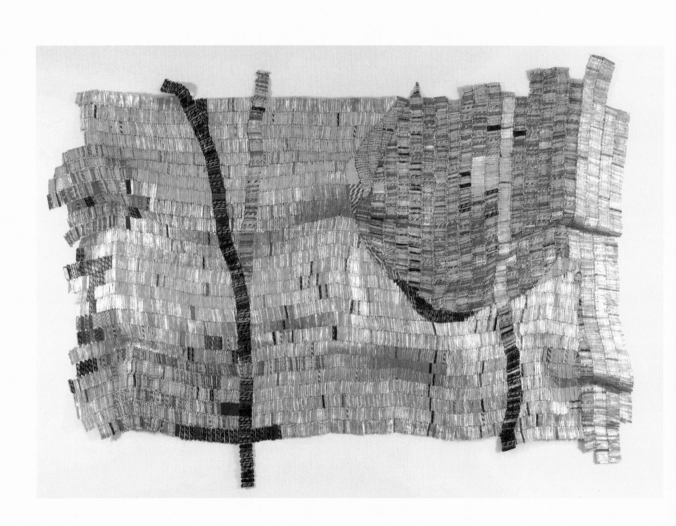

Sacred Moon
2007

67
Bottletop Magic
El Anatsui

The door opens. It's El Anatsui. Inside the big shed, lots of us assistants are working hard. Yes! It may sound like we are talking and laughing. But we are working hard! This is what El Anatsui does. He drives to the studio. He parks round the corner and walks to the door, so we cannot hear him coming.

'What's all this chatter?' he says. 'Art is something spiritual. You must be quiet and concentrate.'

'We are quiet,' we say, quietly. Is he angry? No! He is smiling, because art is something you do with a joyful spirit.

It is hot and sweaty in here. The rainy season is coming. The sky is covered in a grey cloak. It sags down above Nsukka, ready to burst, like the big sacks in the studio, bulging with bottletops. This is what El Anatsui uses for his work – metal bottletops from rum and beer and whisky bottles. The drinks have all been drunk. The bottles have been thrown away. El Anatsui collects the metal tops.

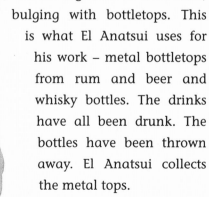

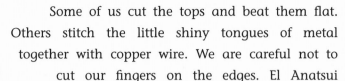

Some of us cut the tops and beat them flat. Others stitch the little shiny tongues of metal together with copper wire. We are careful not to cut our fingers on the edges. El Anatsui keeps a close eye on what we are doing. He'll point out something that we haven't seen. 'Look, you can do it like this,' he'll say. 'All you assistants – it is like conducting an orchestra of musicians,' he tells us.

We make blocks of wired-together bottletops, like metal mats. When enough blocks are ready, we lay them on the floor. Silver, gold, blue, red-striped – all the shiny colours of the bottletops. How should they fit together? This way or that way? El Anatsui decides. Each arrangement, each pattern, has a different meaning. When he has decided, we join the blocks together in one enormous sheet.

El Anatsui hasn't always lived in Nigeria. He grew up in Ghana, with no less than 30 brothers and sisters! At college he read books about African art. The books weren't written by Africans. They made it sound as if the marks and shapes that African artists use are just pretty patterns, like a flowery shirt. It was obvious these writers did not understand *adinkra*.

If you'd grown up in Ghana, you would know about *adinkra* signs. You'd see them every day, painted on walls and clay pots, printed on cloth. There is a sign that looks like a wooden comb, a *duafe*, which means 'beauty'. The sign called *osram ne nsoromma* is the shining sun with the crescent moon under, like a cradle. Its meaning is 'love and harmony'. El Anatsui liked the big meanings that belong to little shapes you can print on a T-shirt or scratch on a piece of wood. He made drawings of *adinkra*, putting them together in different combinations.

All this time he was noticing that roads, pathways, marketplaces and shops, everywhere he went, were covered with rubbish that people had dropped. When he looked more closely, he realised that even the rubbish was covered in signs. They weren't *adinkra*, but they meant something all the same. He picked up a bottletop. It had a blue frilly edge around a white and blue circle. In the middle of the blue circle was a silver star.

He started to collect bottletops. The names on them were like the names in legends or films. Dark Sailor, King Solomon, Makossa, Top Squad. When he'd collected a lot of bottletops, he joined them together with wire. They looked like a shiny metal robe, only instead of *adinkra* they had the names of alcoholic drinks. He joined thousands of bottletops together to make a kind of cloak. If you did not look closely at what it was made from, it looked like a glittering mantle fit for a king.

For many centuries, El Anatsui tells us, Europeans came to Africa and carried away our treasures. They carried away our people as slaves and traded with guns and alcohol. 'Look around you,' he says. Africa is being filled with rubbish from all over the world. Empty bottles, milk tins. He shows us how to take this rubbish and turn it into something beautiful.

For a long time El Anatsui taught at the university in Nsukka. Not many people outside Africa knew about his work. Today he is famous. We are proud to be his assistants. More and more people are asking him to make new work for exhibitions. That's what is keeping us so busy.

Suddenly the lights go off. It's a power cut! The air is the colour of iron. The first heavy raindrops fall. Thunder growls. Soon the electricity generator will start up and the lights will come back on. But for one moment, all around us in the shadows, spread out on the concrete floor, the gleam of silver and gold. It is the magic treasure of El Anatsui.

Sunflower Seeds
2010

68
Sowing Seeds
Ai Weiwei

I've kept my eyes tight shut. I'm trying to guess what my sister put in my palm. 'Come on,' she says. 'You remember.'

Is it a bead? A tooth?

'All right. You can look now.'

It's a tiny, pale object with thin black stripes. A sunflower seed. 'What do think?' she asks. 'I made it from modelling clay and painted it. Guess how long it took.'

I shake my head. 'A whole hour,' she says. 'A *whole hour.*' Then she tells me, 'Ai Weiwei is under house arrest.'

I'd better explain. In 2011, which already feels a long time ago, we went with school to see an art exhibition. It was by an artist called Ai Weiwei. All it was was the floor of a huge hall covered in sunflower seeds. Except they weren't real seeds. There were a hundred million of them, and they were all made – every single one – out of hard white porcelain and painted by hand. My sister said it took 1,600 craftsmen two-and-a-half years to make them all, which added up to four thousand years of making and painting seeds. Every seed was different. 'What's the point?' I whispered, looking at the enormous whitey-grey carpet of seeds.

'The point is …' My sister aways has the answer. 'The point is that every tiny seed is a work of art all on its own. Look,' she knelt and picked one up.

'You're not supposed to touch them,' said the person in charge of the gallery.

Being told off made my sister especially determined to find out more about Ai Weiwei. Which meant that I heard a lot about him too.

Ai Weiwei was born in China. His father was a famous poet, so obviously he had his own ideas about things. The Chinese government didn't like people who thought for themselves. Ai Weiwei's family was sent to a prison camp, then they were forced to live in a far-away corner of China. When Ai Weiwei was 20 he went to film school. After that, he travelled to America. In New York he met poets and artists, and earned money drawing portraits in the street. And he photographed everything. No matter how many thousands of photos he took, each one captured a moment that was completely unique.

In 1993 Ai Weiwei's father fell ill. He decided to go home to China, but he still wanted to share his ideas and his art with people in other countries. This was the time when the internet was just beginning. Ai Weiwei was one the the first artists to use the internet to tell people about his work.

My sister had another go at explaining the sunflower seeds. They stood for Chinese history, she said, because in the town of Jingdezhen where they were made, craftsmen had made porcelain for two thousand years, from the days of the Chinese emperors. And the seeds stood for all the millions and millions of people in the world, because every single person is a unique individual. And they were about Ai Weiwei standing up to the government, which wanted to stop people expressing themselves. 'He says, "Seeds grow ... The crowd will have its way, eventually",' she told me.

I still wasn't sure I understood. I Googled 'Ai Weiwei'. I found a film of him talking about being in prison. He often criticises the Chinese government. Soon after the sunflower seed exhibition, he was arrested and locked up for 81 days. No one would tell him what he'd done wrong. He was released, but now he's not allowed to leave his house.

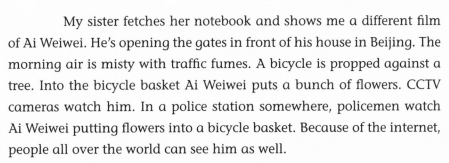

My sister fetches her notebook and shows me a different film of Ai Weiwei. He's opening the gates in front of his house in Beijing. The morning air is misty with traffic fumes. A bicycle is propped against a tree. Into the bicycle basket Ai Weiwei puts a bunch of flowers. CCTV cameras watch him. In a police station somewhere, policemen watch Ai Weiwei putting flowers into a bicycle basket. Because of the internet, people all over the world can see him as well.

I can't understand what he's done wrong either. He helped to design the amazing 'bird's nest' stadium for the Beijing Olympics, but that didn't seem to make the government pleased with him. He doesn't look like a trouble-maker. He wears plain grey clothes, like a factory worker. He has a straggly beard and his face looks serious, yet his eyes laugh easily.

And here's another film. Ai Weiwei is talking about the sunflower seeds. He is pushing the rake backwards and forwards across the floor of a big room covered with porcelain seeds. 'Sometimes people try to taste them,' he says. Here's a photo of him that I like. He's looking straight at us, holding out his cupped hands. They are filled with sunflower seeds. 'It's simple,' he seems to say. 'These are for sharing. Go on. Take one.'

Map of the World

This map shows the locations of many of the places featured in the book. Country borders have changed over the 40,000 years covered by the book, but this map shows where places are today.

Arctic Ocean

Rocky Mountains

New York

United States of America

Mexico

Pacific Ocean

Atlantic Ocean

Atlas Mountains

Niger

Andes

Southern Ocean

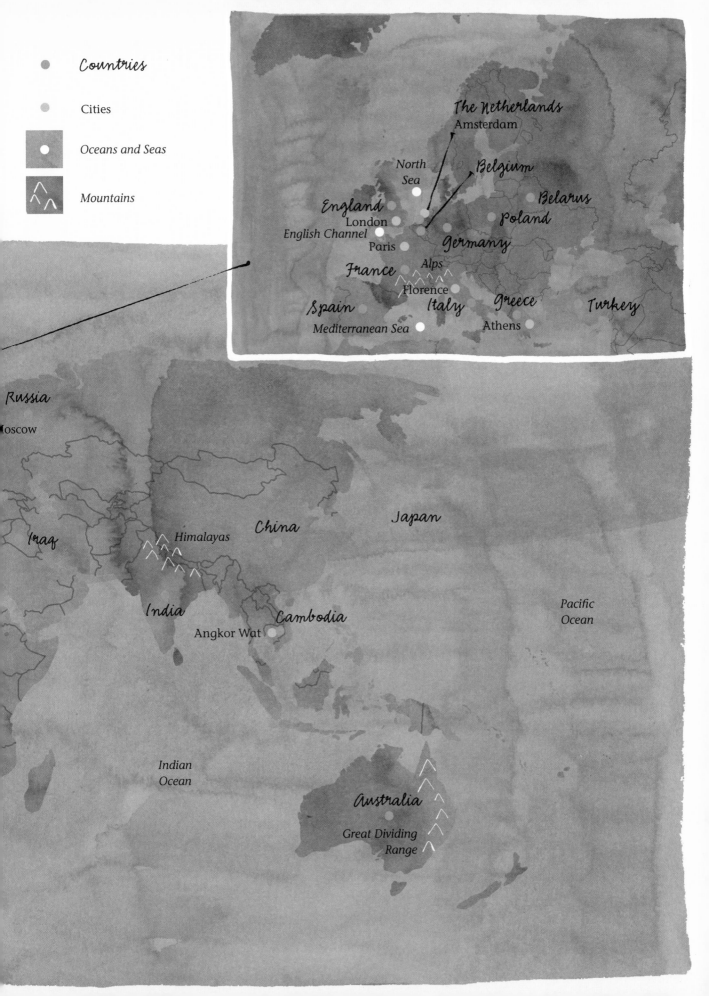

Timeline

Dates are in the form of either BCE or CE. These letters stand for 'Before the Common Era' and 'Common Era'. CE begins with the year when Jesus is thought to have been born and then works forwards, up to today. BCE starts at the same point and works backwards. The letters CE are not usually added to a date when it's obvious that it is 'Common Era'. Sometimes it seems easier to say 'about 5,000 years ago' than 'about 3000 BCE', but historians mostly prefer to use BCE and CE.

People, places and artworks that you can read about in the stories in this book are marked in **bold**.

You can look up words that are underlined in the glossary.

108,000–10,000 BCE
The Ice Age.

About 40,000–35,000 BCE
The figure known as the **Lion Man** is carved from mammoth tusk in what is now Germany.

About 32,000–30,000 BCE
Figures of **horses, bison and rhinoceros** are painted on a wall of Chauvet Cave in France.

About 10,000–7,000 BCE
Farming develops in the Nile Valley, the Middle East and other regions when people begin to domesticate animals and cultivate food crops.

About 4000–3000 BCE
The world's first cities grow up in the Middle East, with city walls, temples and palaces.

About 3200 BCE
Writing is developed for keeping records in Iraq and (probably slightly later) in Egypt, where a form of picture writing called hieroglyphs is used.

About 1390 BCE
The **Tomb of Menna** is built and decorated with paintings in Egypt.

About 1353–1336 BCE
An Egyptian sculptor makes a relief carving of **Akhenaten and his family**.

About 1320 BCE
Tutankhamun's mummy is buried in a **painted tomb** in the Valley of the Kings, Egypt.

About 575–560 BCE
The Greek vase painter **Kleitias** paints scenes from myths and legends on a large **wine vase** made by the potter **Ergotimos** in Athens.

447–432 BCE
The temple of the goddess Athena, called the **Parthenon**, is built on the hill of the Acropolis in Athens, Greece. The sculptor **Phidias** is in charge of the sculptures on the Parthenon, including the **horses** of the sun and moon.

228–210 BCE
An army of life-size terracotta **warriors** is constructed to guard the tomb of **Emperor Qin Shi Huang** in China.

146 BCE
The Roman army conquers Greece.

27 BCE
The Roman leader Octavian declares himself emperor and takes the name Augustus.

About 20 BCE
A **statue of Emperor Augustus** is sculpted in Rome. The dining room of the **villa of Livia**, wife of Augustus, is painted with frescoes.

About 0–300 CE
The religion of Christianity, based on the teachings of Jesus, gains followers until it becomes one of the main religions of the Roman Empire.

324 CE
Emperor Constantine founds the city of Constantinople (today called Istanbul).

410 CE
Rome is attacked and ransacked by an army of Visigoths from northern Europe.

About 400–1400
The Middle Ages in Europe.

About 400–600
Christianity continues to spread through Europe.

About 610–632
The Prophet Muhammad establishes the religion of Islam.

867
The mosaic of the **Virgin Mary and Jesus Christ** is finished in the Church of Saint Sophia, Constantinople (now Istanbul, Turkey).

1001
The calligrapher Ibn al-Bawwab writes out a new copy of the **Qur'an** in Baghdad.

About 990–1020
The Chinese artist **Fan Kuan** paints a hanging scroll with a scene of **travellers among mountains and streams**.

About 1120–50
The temple of **Angkor Wat** is built in Cambodia. The walls are covered with carvings, including a scene of a **king riding into battle on an elephant**.

1194
Chartres Cathedral in northern France burns down and the building of a new cathedral begins.

About 1194–1250
More than 170 stained-glass windows are created for the new Chartres Cathedral, including a window with traditional scenes of the **Labours of the Months**.

1296
Building work begins on a new cathedral in Florence, Italy.

About 1305
The Italian artist **Giotto** finishes his wall paintings in the **Scrovegni Chapel** (also called the Arena Chapel) in Padua, including a picture of *The Expulsion of the Money-Changers from the Temple*.

About 1325
The city of Tenochtitlán (present-day Mexico City) is founded by the Aztec, or Mexica, people in Mexico.

About 1325–35
A scribe and several illuminators (artists) in eastern England create the **Luttrell Book of Psalms** for Sir Geoffrey Luttrell.

About 1300–1400
Yoruba metalsmiths in Ife in west Africa cast the **head of a king**.

About 1400–1600
The Renaissance (meaning 'rebirth') in European art and culture takes place, first in Italy and then in other regions.

1418
The Italian artist and architect **Filippo Brunelleschi** wins a competition to design the dome of **Florence Cathedral**. Among Brunelleschi's other ideas is a new method of perspective for showing three-dimensional space in two-dimensional pictures.

1423–25
Donatello creates the bronze relief *The Feast of Herod* for the baptistery font in Siena Cathedral, central Italy.

About 1425–27
The Russian monk and icon painter **Andrei Rublev** paints *The Three Angels*.

1434
Jan van Eyck paints the *Portrait of Giovanni Arnolfini and His Wife* in the city of Bruges (now in Belgium).

1436
The dome of **Florence Cathedral** is finally completed, 140 years after building work began on the new cathedral.

About 1440
Under the Aztec ruler Moctezuma, work begins on rebuilding the **Great Temple** at Tenochtitlán for the fourth time.

1450–56
The German goldsmith Johann Gutenberg experiments with movable metal type (single letters of the alphabet that can be arranged in any combination for printing). He prints a two-volume Bible, the first full-length book ever printed.

About 1480
Terracotta statues of **Eagle Knights** installed at the Great Temple at Tenochtitlán.

About 1490
Leonardo da Vinci paints *The Lady with the Ermine (Cecilia Gallerani)* in Milan, Italy.

1492
The Italian explorer Cristoforo Colombo (Christopher Columbus) crosses the Atlantic Ocean to the Bahamas, leading to regular contact between Europe and America.

1495
The German artist **Albrecht Dürer** travels to Italy for the first time, painting watercolours of the places he passes through between Nuremberg and Venice.

1501–4
Michelangelo sculpts *David* in Florence.

1503
Albrecht Dürer paints *The Great Piece of Turf*.

1505
Michelangelo is summoned by Pope Julius the Second to Rome, where he designs a grand tomb for the pope and paints the ceiling of the **Sistine Chapel**.

1508
Raphael is summoned to Rome by Pope Julius.

1510–12
Raphael paints *Philosophy, or The School of Athens*, one of a set of paintings for the pope's library in the Vatican Palace in Rome.

1520–23
Titian paints *Bacchus and Ariadne* for Alfonso, Duke of Ferrara.

1521
Tenochtitlán is devastated by the army of Hernán Cortés, leader of a Spanish expedition to Mexico. During the next 50 years, Mexico and much of South America are invaded and colonised by Spain and Portugal.

About 1551
The artist **Pieter Bruegel** leaves Flanders (now part of Belgium) and travels to Italy, where he spends about three years studying Italian art.

1565
Bruegel paints *Hunters in the Snow* as one of a set of paintings for the merchant **Nicolaes Jonghelinck**'s house in Antwerp (now in Belgium).

1589
In India, Emperor Akbar commands his friend the scholar Abu'l Fazl to write the history of his reign, the **Book of Akbar**.

About 1590–95
Basawan and **Dharm Das** paint *Akbar Hunts in the Neighbourhood of Agra*, one of many illustrations for the **Book of Akbar**.

1601
The Italian artist **Caravaggio** paints *The Supper at Emmaus* in Rome for his patron Ciriaco Mattei.

1602
The Dutch East India Company founded in Amsterdam, which becomes one of Europe's richest trading centres.

1606
Caravaggio is forced to flee from Rome after killing Ranuccio Tommasoni in a fight.

1610
Caravaggio dies on his way back from Naples to Rome.

1623
Diego Velázquez paints his first portrait of **King Philip the Fourth** of Spain.

1631
The Dutch artist **Rembrandt van Rijn** leaves his hometown of Leiden and settles in **Amsterdam** (now in the Netherlands).

1635
Rembrandt paints a portrait of his wife, *Saskia van Uylenburgh in Arcadian Costume*.

1638–39
The Italian artist **Artemisia Gentileschi** paints *Self-Portrait as the Allegory of Painting*, probably during a visit to London.

1642–51
The English Civil War. King Charles the First is executed in 1649.

1648
Royal Academy of Painting and Sculpture founded in Paris.

1656
Velázquez paints *The Maids of Honour*.

1664
Claude Lorrain paints *Landscape with Psyche outside the Palace of Cupid* (also known as *The Enchanted Castle*).

1667
The first Salon exhibition is staged by the French Royal Academy of Painting and Sculpture. The Salon becomes a regular event in Paris until the late nineteenth century.

About 1669–70
The Dutch artist **Johannes Vermeer** paints *The Love Letter* in Delft.

1670s
Antonie van Leeuwenhoek makes many discoveries with his home-made microscopes in Delft.

1728
Jean-Siméon Chardin is elected a member of the French Royal Academy.

About 1736–37
Chardin paints *The House of Cards*.

About 1760–1840
The Industrial Revolution in Europe. Steam-powered machines, large factories and railways change the way people live. Towns and cities grow rapidly.

1768
Royal Academy of Arts founded in London.

1778
At the age of 19, the Japanese artist **Katsushika Hokusai** begins his long career as a maker of woodblock prints.

1786
The Spanish artist **Francisco de Goya** becomes the King of Spain's official painter.

1789
The French Revolution begins. Revolutionary forces storm the Bastille prison in Paris.

1793
Maximilien Robespierre argues that King Louis the Sixteenth of France deserves the death penalty. King Louis is executed in Paris. **Jacques-Louis David** paints *The Death of Marat*.

1799
The French general **Napoleon Bonaparte** seizes control of the government.

1803–15
The Napoleonic Wars in Europe. Under Napoleon's leadership, the French army invades Austria, Russia, Spain and other regions. The years of conflict end with Napoleon's final defeat at the Battle of Waterloo in 1815.

1807
The British artist **Joseph Mallord William Turner** becomes Professor of Perspective at the Royal Academy in London.

1808
The people of Madrid attack the French troops who have entered their city.

1813
Napoleon's forces occupy the German city of Dresden. The artist **Caspar David Friedrich** takes refuge in the mountains nearby.

1814
Goya paints *The 3rd of May 1808 (Execution of the Defenders of Madrid)* in Spain.

About 1818
Friedrich paints *The Wayfarer above a Sea of Fog*.

1831
Hokusai makes his print *The Great Wave off Kanagawa*, one of his *Thirty-Six Views of Mount Fuji*.

About 1833
William Henry Fox Talbot begins to experiment in England with chemical processes that will lead to **photography**. He places leaves and flowers on light-sensitive paper, capturing images without a camera.

1841
Using a camera, **Talbot** takes the first of several photographs of an open door and a broom at his home, Lacock Abbey.

1842
Turner paints *Snow Storm – Steam-Boat off a Harbour's Mouth* and exhibits it at the Royal Academy.

1844
Talbot takes his last and best-known photograph of *The Open Door*.

1851
The French artist **Gustave Courbet** exhibits three paintings at the Salon in Paris. Visitors are shocked to see large-scale paintings of labourers and peasants going about their everyday work.

1853
The American artist **Frederic Edwin Church** travels to the Andes Mountains in South America, making many sketches. On returning to New York, Church creates large paintings from these sketches.

1854
Courbet paints *The Meeting*.

1857
Church paints *Niagara* and exhibits it in a gallery in New York, where people pay to see it.

1861–65
The American Civil War.

1868
The English photographer **Eadweard Muybridge** (born Edward James Muggeridge) publishes his book of American photographs *Scenery of the Yosemite Valley*.

1872
The French artist **Berthe Morisot** paints *The Cradle*.

1874

Berthe Morisot, Claude Monet and Paul Cézanne are among thirty artists involved in the First Impressionist Exhibition in Paris. Monet exhibits his painting *Impression, Sunrise*, after which the Impressionists are named.

1877

Monet paints *Saint-Lazare Station* in Paris.

1878

Muybridge makes the photographic series ***The Horse in Motion*** in the United States.

1879

The art student **Georges Seurat** visits the Fourth Impressionist Exhibition in Paris.

About 1884

The French sculptor **Camille Claudel** begins to assist **Auguste Rodin** with his huge sculptural project *The Gates of Hell*.

1884–86

Seurat paints *A Sunday on the Island of La Grande Jatte*, using his new technique of pointillism.

1886

The Dutch artist **Vincent van Gogh** moves to Paris.

About 1887

Cézanne paints ***Sainte-Victoire Mountain with Large Pine*** near Aix-en-Provence, France.

1889

The Universal Exposition is held in Paris. The exposition presents cultural and industrial achievements from across the world. Its centrepiece is the newly completed Eiffel Tower.

1889

Van Gogh paints ***The Starry Night*** in Saint-Rémy, France.

1897–1903

Claudel sculpts *The Wave*.

1904–6

Cézanne and the artist Emile Bernard exchange letters.

1905

Henri Matisse and other young artists are branded 'Fauves' (wild beasts) when they exhibit their brightly coloured paintings in Paris.

1907

Georges Braque visits the studio of **Pablo Picasso** in Paris, where he is impressed by Picasso's strange new painting.

The two artists begin to work together. They develop a new type of art that becomes known as Cubism.

1909

The Russian artist **Vasily Kandinsky** begins to make abstract paintings, in which the shapes, lines and colours no longer represent recognisable objects.

1910

After studying art in St Petersburg, Russia, **Marc Chagall** goes to Paris.

About 1910–11

Varvara Stepanova and **Aleksandr Rodchenko** meet while studying at Kazan School of Art in Russia.

1912

Picasso makes *Still-life with Chair Caning* in Paris.

1913

The French artist **Marcel Duchamp** creates his first 'ready-made' work of art, ***Bicycle Wheel***.

1914

Braque makes his collage ***The Violin***. In August war breaks out and he is called up to serve in the French army.

1914–18

First World War.

1915

In his hometown Vitebsk in Belarus, **Chagall** paints ***Birthday***. **Duchamp** leaves France for New York. He buys a snow shovel and hangs it in his studio as another 'ready-made' work of art.

1917

The Russian Revolution. The end of rule by the tsar (emperor) and the first Communist government, led by Vladimir Lenin.

1919

The **Bauhaus** school of art, architecture and design founded in Weimar, Germany.

1920

The Spanish artist **Joan Miró** moves to Paris, where he later associates with Surrealist artists.

1921

The First Working Group of Constructivists set up in Moscow. Its members include **Stepanova** and **Rodchenko**.

1922
Tutankhamun's Tomb rediscovered in Egypt.

1923
In Russia, **Stepanova** creates her **designs for sports clothing**. In Germany, **Kurt Schwitters** begins constructing his *Merzbau* out of rubbish. It eventually takes up much of the space in his home and studio.

1924
The French writer André Breton publishes *The Surrealist Manifesto*. He explains that Surrealism means art that expresses a person's inner thoughts and dreams without any control by reason.

1925
The **Bauhaus** moves from Weimar to a new building in Dessau, Germany, constructed in glass and concrete in a modern style.

1926
Kandinsky paints *Several Circles*.

1932
The Mexican artist **Frida Kahlo** paints *Self-Portrait on the Border between Mexico and the United States*.

1933
Adolf Hitler, leader of the Nazi party, becomes Chancellor of Germany.

1933–34
Miró paints *Hirondelle Amour*.

1936–39
Spanish Civil War.

1937
Picasso paints *Guernica* in Paris.

1938
The French artist **Louise Bourgeois** moves to New York.

1939
Fragments of prehistoric sculpture known as the **Lion Man** discovered in a cave in Germany.

1939–45
Second World War.

1940–41
Henry Moore sketches in the London Underground during air raids, producing many drawings, including *Three Figures Sleeping*.

1943
The German city of Hanover is bombed by British and American planes, destroying **Schwitters's** *Merzbau*.

1945
Atomic bombs are dropped by American planes on the Japanese cities of Hiroshima and Nagasaki.

1947
The American artist **Jackson Pollock** makes his first drip paintings, including *Full Fathom Five*.

1948–51
Matisse creates the stained-glass window *Tree of Life* for the chapel in the town of Vence in France.

About 1974
The German artist **Anselm Kiefer** starts to use lead in his work. He later makes books with lead pages, representing the 'weight of history'.

1975
The Ghanaian artist **El Anatsui** starts to make work using traditional adinkra signs.

1981
Kiefer creates *Landscape with Wing*. The Chinese artist Ai Weiwei moves to New York.

1981–88
The Australian Aboriginal artist **Emily Kame Kngwarreye** makes batik textiles.

1989
Kngwarreye paints *Ntange Dreaming* in Utopia, Australia.

1993
Bourgeois creates *Cell (Choisy)*. **Ai Wewei** returns to Beijing, China.

1994
Chauvet Cave is discovered by explorers in France.

2007
El Anatsui creates the wall hanging *Sacred Moon* in Nsukka, Nigeria.

2010
Ai Weiwei creates *Sunflower Seeds*. In Beijing Ai Wewei is arrested. In 2015 he is allowed to travel outside China again and has an exhibition in London.

Glossary

abstract Art that uses shapes, lines and areas of colour rather than recognisable figures or images.

adinkra Traditional West African signs with meanings such as welcome, hope, strength and love.

allegory Using a figure or object to stand for an idea, like the Statue of Liberty.

architect Someone who designs buildings.

aristocrat A member of the aristocracy, the hereditary ruling class.

azure A bright, clear blue, like the blue of the sky.

baptistery Area of a church used for a baptism, a ceremony in which young children (and sometimes adults) are sprinkled or covered with water as a symbol of becoming a Christian.

barbarian A name for someone who is considered very uncivilised.

batik A method of making patterns on cloth by painting it with wax, then dyeing it.

Bauhaus A school of art and design in Germany in the early twentieth century; also the name for the modern, geometric style of design associated with the Bauhaus.

Bible The holy book of Christianity.

bronze A metal made by melting copper with a small amount of tin and other metals such as zinc.

bronze relief A bronze sculpture in which shapes stick out from a flat background, forming a three-dimensional picture.

camera A device that focuses a very narrow beam of light onto a surface that reacts to light, so that a photographic image is formed.

calligraphy The art of beautiful handwriting, often practised with ink and a pen or brush.

canvas A surface for painting on, made from a piece of strong cloth (called canvas) stretched tightly over a frame.

casting Pouring a molten metal such as bronze into a mould to make a shaped object or sculpture.

cave painting A picture on the inside walls of a cave, usually painted in prehistoric times.

charcoal A stick of charred wood, which can be used for drawing.

chisel A sharp tool, hit with a hammer or wooden mallet to cut into stone or wood.

Christianity A world religion based on the life and teachings of Jesus, written down in the Bible.

civilisation A highly organised society with cities, a code of laws, and cultural achievements such as works of art, literature, music and grand buildings.

clay Fine-grained, sticky soil that can be shaped and fired (baked) to make pottery.

collage Sticking pieces of paper or other materials onto a flat surface to make a picture, which is called a collage.

commission To ask someone to make a piece of art or do other work in return for payment.

Constructivism An art movement that flourished after the Russian Revolution, in which artists saw themselves as helping to construct a new society, along with architects, designers and others.

critic Someone whose job is to comment on or write about art, music, books, drama and other art forms.

Cubism An art movement that began in Paris in the early twentieth century. Cubism involved using several different viewpoints to create one picture or sculpture.

design The process of deciding and planning how something will look or work, which often starts by making drawings.

designer Someone who designs things, such as furniture, household items, machines or clothes.

drip painting A method of painting by dripping paint, for example from a tin or a stick, onto a flat surface.

easel An upright frame on legs, for holding a painting or other artwork that is being worked on or displayed. The word *easel* comes from the Dutch word for a donkey.

ebony A type of hard black or dark brown wood from the tropical ebony tree.

Egyptian blue A blue pigment made by mixing copper, lime and other minerals. It has been used since ancient Egyptian times.

embalmer Someone who prepares dead bodies for burial. Ancient Egyptian embalmers used their skills to turn bodies into mummies.

engineer A person who designs or builds machines or large structures such as roads and bridges.

exhibition A public display of artworks or other interesting items.

Fauvism An art movement in early-twentieth-century France that used bold shapes and bright, unnatural-looking colours for figures and objects. The name comes from the French word *fauves*, meaning 'wild beasts'.

figure A human form depicted in a painting or other work of art.

firing Baking clay objects at high temperatures to harden them into pottery.

flint A type of hard stone that can be chipped and sharpened to make tools.

fresco A method of painting directly onto on wet plaster on a wall or ceiling, so that the paint combines with the plaster. The paintings themselves are called frescoes; the name comes from the Italian word for 'fresh'.

gold leaf Gold beaten into a extremely thin sheets, which can be used by artists to create areas of pure gold in their pictures.

goldsmith Someone who makes jewellery or other objects out of gold and other precious metals.

guappo Italian slang word for a boaster or bully.

guillotine Machine containing a heavy blade that slides downwards. It was used for beheading people in public during the French Revolution.

hieroglyph A picture-sign that stands for a thing, idea, word or sound.

icon A traditional Christian image, usually painted on a wooden panel.

illumination Decorating the pages of a book with painted pictures or patterns, often around the edges of the page or as part of the lettering.

Impressionism A movement in painting that began in late-nineteenth-century France. The Impressionists wanted to capture the momentary impression of a scene rather than all its details.

inkstone A piece of stone used for mixing powdered ink and water for painting or writing.

Islam A world religion based on the teachings of the Prophet Muhammad, written down in the Qur'an.

ivory Hard, whitish material made from the tusks of elephants and some other mammals, which was often used in the past for carving.

Jewish Belonging to the Jewish people or to the religion of Judaism.

kiln Very hot oven for firing pottery.

Labours of the Months A set of pictures of the different kinds of work in the fields and other activities that were associated with each month in the Middle Ages. For example, keeping warm by the fire in February, pruning grape vines in March and making hay in June. The Labours of the Months often included pictures of the 12 zodiac signs, such as Pisces (two fish, March–April) and Leo (the lion, July–August).

landscape A picture of a landscape or countryside scene.

lapis lazuli A blue rock that can be ground into powder to make an intense blue pigment for painting.

lead A very heavy, soft metal, used in building and sometimes in art.

lens A piece of curved glass used in magnifying glasses, microscopes and cameras.

limestone A pale rock that is good for carving and is often used for sculptures and buildings.

marble A very hard form of limestone, which has been popular with sculptors and architects since ancient times.

mercury A silvery metal that is liquid at room temperature.

metalsmith A person who is skilled at making things out of metal.

microscope An instrument containing a lens, or lenses, for looking at very small objects, which appear much bigger than they really are.

mosaic A pattern or image made up of very small pieces of hard materials such as stone, glass and pottery.

mould A hollow shape that can be filled with molten metal, liquid plaster or another material, which then hardens and is removed from the mould.

mummy A dead body that is cleaned, treated with oils and chemicals, and wrapped in cloth to preserve it.

mural A large picture painted directly onto a wall.

oil paint Paint made of powdered pigments mixed with vegetable oil, which takes a long time to dry out fully.

onyx A hard stone with bands of different colours.

patron A person who supports or pays an artist to make art.

pediment The triangular area on the front and back of Greek temples and similar buildings, under the two sloping sides of the roof – a good space for groups of statues.

perspective A method of making flat images look three-dimensional, creating the illusion that the foreground in a picture is separated from the background by real distance.

philosophy The study of questions such as 'What is reality?', 'What is the meaning of right and wrong?' and 'What is beauty?' The word *philosophy* comes from the ancient Greek term for 'love of wisdom'.

pigment A substance that produces colour for making paint, dyeing textiles or other uses. For example, red paint can be made from a mineral called red ochre.

plaster A powdered substance mixed with water which hardens as its dries. It is used for applying a smooth coating to rough walls and sometimes for making sculptures.

pointillism Painting with lots of tiny dots of colour, putting different coloured dots next to each other, instead of using long strokes of the brush. This method was developed by the French artist Georges Seurat.

pope The head of the Catholic Church, which is one of the main forms of Christianity. The pope lives in the Vatican Palace in Rome.

porcelain A type of fine, hard, white pottery, first made in China more than two thousand years ago.

portrait A picture or sculpture of a real individual, rather than an imaginary person.

potter Someone who is skilled at making pottery.

potter's wheel A flat, circular board that can be turned by the potter like a wheel. The potter places a lump of clay in the centre of the wheel and shapes it with his or her hands as it spins round.

pottery Pots, plates, figurines or other objects made from clay that is then fired in a kiln.

print To transfer pictures or marks, including words, onto a surface by pressure. For example, woodblock prints are made by carving a flat block of wood, covering the carved block with a layer of ink, and pressing a sheet of paper onto it.

Prussian blue A deep blue chemical used as a pigment in painting and printing. Prussian blue was first produced in Germany in the eighteenth century.

quarry A large pit or a cut-away hillside where stone or other materials are extracted.

Qur'an The holy book of the religion of Islam.

rabbi A teacher or leader in the religion of Judaism.

relief A picture made by carving into a flat surface so that figures and patterns stand out from the background.

retablo A religious picture painted on a small sheet of metal, popular in Mexico.

revolution A far-reaching change in government and the way society is organised, which may be rapid and violent, as in the French Revolution and Russian Revolution. The word *revolution* can also refer to great changes in other areas of life, such as art, technology, agriculture and industry.

roundel A circular area filled with an image or pattern, such as a round picture in a stained-glass window.

sable A species of marten whose dark fur can be used to make fine paintbrushes.

Salon The official art exhibition of the French Royal Academy of Painting and Sculpture in Paris.

sarcophagus A large stone coffin or container for a smaller coffin.

scribe A trained writer who writes out texts by hand, sometimes adding decorations or illustrations.

scroll A long strip of paper or textile that has writing or pictures on it and can be rolled up for storage.

sculptor An artist who makes sculptures.

sculpture A three-dimensional figure or object created by a sculptor; also the art of making sculptures.

self-portrait An artist's portrait of himself or herself.

shrine A place or structure associated with a particular deity or holy person.

shutter The part of a camera that opens and closes quickly to take a picture.

silver nitrate A pale chemical that turns dark when exposed to light, used in photography.

sketch A drawing done quickly on the spot, perhaps outdoors or to jot down an idea. Artists sometimes make a series of sketches in preparation for a more finished artwork.

stained glass Coloured glass used to make windows containing patterns or pictures.

statue A free-standing sculpture of a person or animal.

still life A picture of objects such as fruit, flowers or household items. A still life picture usually focuses on a limited area, like a tabletop.

studio A room or building where an artist works.

sunk relief A type of relief where the carved shapes do not project above the flat surface of the stone or wood. Ancient Egyptian sculptors were skilled in carving sunk reliefs.

Surrealism An art movement that began in Europe in the early twentieth century. The word *surrealism* means 'beyond realism'. Surrealist artists turn to dreams, imagination and fantasy for their ideas.

terracotta A type of pottery that usually turns a reddish colour when fired. Terracotta is not nearly as hard and watertight as porcelain but it has many more uses, from statues to cooking pots to drainpipes. It can be glazed (covered with a mixture of chemicals that forms a thin, glassy coating during firing) to make it watertight.

text Writing, such as the words in a book or on a scroll.

Theotokos A Greek word meaning the Mother of God. In the Christian religion it is a name given to Mary, the mother of Jesus.

vase painting Painting on a pottery container. Ancient Greek vase paintings often feature human figures and mythological scenes.

vellum Thin sheets made from calf skin, used in Europe for writing or painting on before paper became available.

vermilion A deep orange-red colour, originally made from the mineral cinnabar.

wall painting A painting made directly onto a wall.

woodblock A flat block of hard wood, which can have an image carved into it. The woodblock is then used to print the image onto paper.

zoopraxiscope An early machine for projecting pictures that appeared to move, invented by photographer Eadweard Muybridge.

List of Artworks

1 *Lion Man*,
about 40,000–35,000 BCE
From Stadel Cave, Germany
Mammoth ivory
Height 29.6 cm (11⅝ in.)
Museum der Stadt, Ulm,
Germany

2 *Horses, Bison and Rhinoceroses*,
about 32,000–30,000 BCE
Cave painting
Chauvet Cave, Vallon-Pont-
d'Arc, Ardèche Gorge, France

3 *Agricultural Scenes*,
about 1390 BCE
Wall painting
Tomb of Menna, Thebes, Egypt

4 *Akhenaten and His Family*,
about 1353–1336 BCE
From Akhetaten (present-day
Tell el-Amarna), Egypt
Relief carving; stone
31.1 x 38.7 cm (12¼ x 15¼ in.)
Staatliche Museen zu Berlin,
Preussischer Kulturbesitz,
Ägyptisches Museum, Berlin

5 *Burial Chamber, Tomb of
Tutankhamun*,
about 1320 BCE
Valley of the Kings, Thebes, Egypt

6 *Wine Vase with Scenes from
Greek Myths (The Francois Vase)*,
about 575–560 BCE
Made by Ergotimos
(Greek, flourished 575–560 BCE),
painted by Kleitias
(Greek, flourished 575–560 BCE)
Ceramic
Height 66 cm (26 in.)
Museo Archeologico, Florence

7 *Head of a Horse*, 438–432 BCE
From the Parthenon,
Athens, Greece
Marble
Length 83.3 cm (32¾ in.),
height 62.6 cm (24⅝ in.),
width 33.3 cm (13⅛ in.)
British Museum, London

8 *Terracotta Army*, 228–210 BCE
Terracotta
Life-size; various heights
Mausoleum of Qin Shi Huang,
Xi'an, Shaanxi Province, China

9 *Emperor Augustus (Augustus
of Prima Porta)*, about 20 BCE
From Rome, Italy
Marble
Height 2 m (6 ft. 7⅞ in.)
Vatican Museums and Galleries,
Vatican City

10 *Painted Garden*, about 20 BCE
Fresco
Villa of Livia, Prima Porta, Italy

11 *The Virgin Mary and
Jesus Christ*, 867
Mosaic; glass, marble, paint
Church of Saint Sophia,
Constantinople (present-day
Istanbul), Turkey

12 *Qur'an*, 1001
Calligraphy by Ibn al-Bawwab
(Persian, died about 1022)
Manuscript; ink and gold on
buff paper
Each page 17.1 x 13.3 cm
(6¾ x 5¼ in.)
Chester Beatty Library, Dublin

13 Fan Kuan
(Chinese, about 960–1030)
*Travellers among Mountains and
Streams*, about 990–1020
Hanging scroll; ink and light
colours on silk
206.3 x 103.3 cm (81¼ x 40⅝ in.)
National Palace Museum, Taipei

14 *The King Riding into Battle on
an Elephant*, about 1120–50
Stone frieze
Angkor Wat, Cambodia

15 *Stained-Glass Window*,
1194–1250
Glass and lead
February Zodiac window,
panel 5, South Ambulatory
Chartres Cathedral, France

16 Giotto
(Italian, about 1266–1337)
*The Expulsion of the Money-Changers
from the Temple*, about 1305
Fresco
Scrovegni (Arena) Chapel,
Padua, Italy

17 *The Luttrell Book of Psalms*,
about 1325–35
From Lincolnshire, England
Manuscript page; painted parch-
ment with gold and silver embel-
lishment and leather binding
35 x 24.5 cm (13¾ x 9⅝ in.)
British Library, London

18 *Head of a King*, 1300–1400
From Ife, Africa
Bronze
Height 29 cm (11⅜ in.)
National Museum, Lagos,
Nigeria

19 Andrei Rublev
(Russian, about 1370–1430)
The Three Angels, about 1425–27
Tempera on panel
141 x 131 cm (55½ x 44½ in.)
Tretyakov Gallery, Moscow

20 Donatello
(Italian, 1386–1466)
Herod's Feast, 1423–25
Relief; gilded bronze
60 x 60 cm (23⅝ x 23⅝ in.)
Baptistry, Siena Cathedral, Italy

21 Jan van Eyck
(Belgian, about 1390–1441)
*Portrait of Giovanni Arnolfini and
His Wife*, 1434
Oil on oak
82.2 x 60 cm (32⅜ x 23⅝ in.)
The National Gallery, London

22 *Eagle Knight*, about 1480
Stucco and terracotta
Height 170 cm (66⅞ in.)
From the Great Temple,
Tenochtitlán, Mexico,
Aztec civilisation
Museo del Templo Mayor,
Mexico City

23 Leonardo da Vinci
(Italian, 1452–1519)
*The Lady with the Ermine
(Cecilia Gallerani)*, about 1490
Oil on walnut panel
53.4 x 39.3 cm (21 x 15½ in.)
Czartoryski Museum, Cracow,
Poland

24 Albrecht Dürer
(German, 1471–1528)
The Great Piece of Turf, 1503
Bodycolours, heightened with
opaque white on vellum
40.8 x 31.5 cm (16 x 12⅜ in.)
Graphische Sammlung
Albertina, Vienna, Austria

25 Michelangelo
 (Italian, 1475–1564)
David, 1501–4
Marble
Height 5.2 m (17 ft.)
Galleria dell' Accademia,
Florence

26 Raphael
(Italian, 1483–1520)
*Philosophy, or The School
of Athens*, 1510–12
Fresco
5 x 7.7 m (16 ft. 4⅞ in. x
25 ft. 3 in.)
Stanza della Segnatura,
Apostolic Palace, Vatican City
Vatican Museums and Galleries,
Vatican City, Italy

27 Titian
(Italian, about 1488–1576)
Bacchus and Ariadne, 1520–23
Oil on canvas (pre-restoration)
176.5 x 191 cm (69½ x 75¼ in.)
The National Gallery, London

28 Pieter Bruegel the Elder
(Dutch, about 1525–1569)
Hunters in the Snow, 1565
Oil on wood panel
117 x 162 cm (46 x 63¾ in.)
Kunsthistorisches Museum,
Vienna, Austria

29 *Akbar Hunts in the
Neighbourhood of Agra*, 1590–95
Page from the Akbarnama
Composition by Basawan
(Indian, 1550–1610),
painting by Dharm Das
(Indian, about 1500–1600)
Opaque watercolour and
gold on paper
Painting 33.5 x 19.6 cm
(13⅛ x 7¾ in.),
page 37.6 x 23 cm (14¾ x 9 in.)
Victoria and Albert Museum,
London

30 Caravaggio
(Italian, 1571–1610)
The Supper at Emmaus, 1601
Oil and tempera on canvas
141 x 196.2 cm (55½ x 77¼ in.)
The National Gallery, London

31 Rembrandt
(Dutch, 1606–1669)
*Saskia van Uylenburgh in Arcadian
Costume*, 1635
Oil on canvas
123.5 x 97.5 cm (48⅝ x 38⅜ in.)
The National Gallery, London

32 Artemisia Gentileschi
(Italian, 1597–about 1651)
*Self-Portrait as the Allegory of
Painting*, 1638–39
Oil on canvas
96.5 x 73.7 cm (38 x 29 in.)
The Royal Collection Trust,
Windsor Castle, England

33 Diego Velázquez
(Spanish, 1599–1660)
The Maids of Honour, 1656
Oil on canvas
3.2 x 2.8 m (10 ft 5 in. x 9 ft)
Museo Nacional del Prado,
Madrid, Spain

34 Claude Lorrain
(French, 1600–1682)
*Landscape with Psyche outside the
Palace of Cupid (The Enchanted
Castle)*, 1664
Oil on canvas
87.1 x 151.3 cm (34¼ x 59½ in.)
The National Gallery, London

35 Johannes Vermeer
(Dutch, 1632–75)
The Love Letter, about 1669–70
Oil on canvas
44 x 38.5 cm (17 x 15¼ in.)
Rijksmuseum, Amsterdam,
The Netherlands

36 Jean-Siméon Chardin
(French, 1699–1779)
The House of Cards,
about 1736–37
Oil on canvas
60.3 x 71.8 cm (23¾ x 28¼ in.)
The National Gallery, London

37 Jacques-Louis David
(French, 1748–1825)
The Death of Marat, 1793
Oil on canvas
165 x 128 cm (65 x 50⅜ in.)
Musées Royaux des Beaux-Arts
de Belgique, Brussels, Belgium

38 Francisco Goya
(Spanish, 1746–1828)
*The 3rd of May 1808 (Execution of
the Defenders of Madrid)*, 1814
Oil on canvas
2.7 x 4.1 m (8 ft. 10¼ in. x
13 ft. 5⅜ in.)
Museo Nacional del Prado,
Madrid, Spain

39 Caspar David Friedrich
(German, 1774–1840)
The Wayfarer above a Sea of Fog,
about 1818
Oil on canvas
98.4 x 74.8 cm (38¾ x 29½ in.)
Hamburger Kunsthalle,
Hamburg, Germany

40 Katsushika Hokusai
(Japanese, 1760–1849)
The Great Wave off Kanagawa,
from the series *Thirty-Six Views of
Mount Fuji*, 1831
Hand-coloured woodblock print
25.7 x 37.9 cm (10⅛ x 14⅞ in.)
The Metropolitan Museum of
Art, New York

41 William Henry Fox Talbot
(English, 1800–1877)
The Open Door, fourth version,
April 1844
Photograph
14.3 x 19.4 cm (5⅝ x 7⅝ in.)
The Metropolitan Museum of
Art, New York

42 Joseph Mallord William
Turner (English, 1775–1851)
*Snow Storm – Steam-Boat off a
Harbour's Mouth*, 1842
Oil on canvas
91.5 x 122 cm (36 x 48 in.)
Tate Britain, London

43 Gustave Courbet
(French, 1819–1877)
The Meeting, 1854
Oil on canvas
129 x 149 cm (50¾ x 58⅝ in.)
Musée Fabre, Montpellier, France

44 Frederic Edwin Church
(American, 1826–1900)
Niagara, 1857
Oil on canvas
101.6 x 229.9 cm (40 x 90½ in.)
Corcoran Gallery of Art,
Washington, D.C.

45 Berthe Morisot
(French, 1841–1895)
The Cradle, 1872
Oil on canvas
56 x 46.5 cm (22 x 18⅛ in.)
Musée d'Orsay, Paris

46 Claude Monet
(French, 1840–1926)
Saint-Lazare Station, 1877
Oil on canvas
75 x 105 cm (29½ x 41¼ in.)
Musée d'Orsay, Paris

47 Eadweard Muybridge
(English, 1830–1904)
The Horse in Motion, from
Horses. Running, 1878–79
Photograph of 24 consecutive
images of a man riding a horse
16 x 22.4 cm (6¼ x 8¾ in.)
Library of Congress

48 Georges Seurat
(French, 1859–1891)
*A Sunday on the Island of
La Grande Jatte*, 1884–86
Oil on canvas
2.1 x 3.1 m (6 ft. 9¾ in. x
10 ft. 1¼ in.)
The Art Institute of Chicago

49 Vincent van Gogh
(Dutch, 1853–1890)
The Starry Night, 1889
Oil on canvas
73.7 x 92.1 cm (29 x 36¼ in.)
Museum of Modern Art,
New York

50 Camille Claudel (French,
1864–1943)
The Wave, 1897–1903
Onyx marble and bronze
62 x 56 cm (24⅜ x 22 in.)
Musée Rodin, Paris

51 Paul Cézanne
(French, 1839–1906)
*Sainte-Victoire Mountain with
Large Pine*, about 1887
Oil on canvas
64.8 x 92.3 cm (25½ x 36¼ in.)
The Courtauld Gallery, London

52 Georges Braque
(French, 1882–1963)
The Violin, early 1914
Cut and pasted papers with
charcoal and graphite
71.8 x 51.8 cm (28¼ x 20⅜ in.)
Cleveland Museum of Art, Ohio

53 Marc Chagall (French,
born in Belarus, 1887–1985)
Birthday, 1915
Oil on cardboard
80.6 x 99.7 cm (31¾ x 39¼ in.)
Museum of Modern Art, New York

54 Marcel Duchamp (American,
born in France, 1887–1968)
Bicycle Wheel, 1951 (copy of the
lost original of 1913)
Metal wheel, painted wood stool
Overall height 128.3 cm (50 in.),
width 63.8 cm (25 in.),
depth 42 cm (16⅝ in.)
Museum of Modern Art, New York

55 Varvara Stepanova
(Russian, 1894–1958)
Designs for Sports Clothing, 1923
Illustrated in *Lef* magazine,
no. 2, 1923

56 Vasily Kandinsky
(Russian, 1866–1944)
Several Circles, 1926
Oil on canvas
140.3 x 140.7 cm (55¼ x 55⅜ in.)
Solomon R. Guggenheim
Museum, New York

57 Frida Kahlo
(Mexican, 1907–1954)
*Self-Portrait on the Border
between Mexico and the
United States*, 1932
Oil on metal
31.8 x 34.9 cm (12½ x 13¾ in.)
Collection of María Rodríguez de
Reyero, New York

58 Joan Miró
(Spanish, 1893–1983)
Hirondelle Amour, 1933–34
Oil on canvas
199.3 x 247.6 cm (78½ x 97½ in.)
Museum of Modern Art, New York

59 Pablo Picasso
(Spanish, 1881–1973)
Guernica, 1937
Oil on canvas
3.5 x 7.8 m (11 ft. 5½ in. x
25 ft. 5¾ in.)
Museo Nacional Centro de Arte
Reina Sofía, Madrid

60 Henry Moore
(British, 1898–1986)
Three Figures Sleeping, study for
Shelter Drawing, 1940–41
Pen, India ink, crayon,
watercolour and wash on paper
34.2 x 48.2 cm (13½ x 19 in.)
Private Collection

61 Kurt Schwitters
(German, 1887–1948)
Merzbau, about 1923–33
(destroyed 1943)
Installation; Paper, cardboard,
plaster, glass, mirrors, metal,
wood, stone, paint, electric
lighting and various other
materials
Height about 3.9 m (12 ft. 9½ in.),
width about 5.8 m (19 ft.),
depth about 4.6 m (14 ft. 11½ in.)
Sprengel Museum, Hanover,
Germany

62 Jackson Pollock
(American, 1912–1956)
Full Fathom Five, 1947
Oil on canvas with nails, tacks,
buttons, key, coins, cigarettes,
matches, etc.
129.2 x 76.5 cm (50⅞ x 30⅛ in.)
Museum of Modern Art, New York

63 Henri Matisse
(French, 1869–1954)
Tree of Life, 1948–51
Stained glass
Chapelle du Rosaire de Vence,
France

64 Anselm Kiefer
(German, born in 1945)
Landscape with Wing, 1981
Oil, straw and lead on canvas
3.3 x 5.5 m (10 ft. 10 in. x 18 ft.)
Virginia Museum of Fine Arts

65 Emily Kame Kngwarreye
(Australian, about 1910–1996)
Ntange Dreaming, 1989
Synthetic polymer paint
on canvas
135 x 122 cm (53⅛ x 48 in.)
National Gallery of Australia,
Canberra

66 Louise Bourgeois
(French, 1911–2010)
Cell (Choisy), 1993
Pink marble, metal and glass
Height 3.6 m (11 ft. 9¾ in.),
width 1.7 m (5 ft. 7 in.),
depth 2.4 m (7 ft. 10½ in.)
Installation at Ydessa Hendeles
Art Foundation, Toronto,
Surrogates, 13 May 1995–
April 1996

67 El Anatsui
(Ghanaian, born in 1944)
Sacred Moon, 2007
Aluminium and copper wire
2.6 x 3.6 m (8 ft. 6 in. x
11 ft. 9¾ in.)
Mott-Warsh Collection, Flint,
Michigan

68 Ai Weiwei
(Chinese, born in 1957)
Sunflower Seeds, 2010
Paint on porcelain
100 million seeds
Installation at Tate Modern,
London, 12 October 2010–
2 May 2011

Index

Credits

The stories in this book are fictionalised accounts inspired by the lives and art of different artists. All quotes are literary inventions unless otherwise noted.

Acknowledgements

Thank you to Laurence King for inviting me to write this book and for his enthusiasm and encouragement throughout. It's been a great pleasure to work with Kate Evans, who has created such lovely, lively illustrations. Thank you, too, to my editors at Laurence King Publishing, Elizabeth Jenner and Jodi Simpson, and to the book's designer, Vanessa Green at The Urban Ant Ltd. The stories gained much from the responses of friends and family to early drafts; I especially thank Helen Dunmore, Will and Lexie, and Felicity, as always.